AI and YOU

Making Sense of Artificial Intelligence

In this insightful book, you'll delve into the countless ways AI is seamlessly integrated into our lives, bringing efficiency, convenience, and boundless possibilities. Discover how smart homes are no longer a distant dream but a tangible reality, where AI-driven virtual assistants anticipate our needs, adjust the environment for optimal comfort, and make everyday tasks effortless.

John A Robinson

Table of Contents

- The rising influence of AI in modern life and its impact on daily routines

- Debunking myths and fears about AI usage

- The objective of the book: empowering the average person to embrace AI and leverage its potential to improve daily life

- Understanding the fundamentals of AI in layman's terms

- The various types of AI and their applications in real-world scenarios

- An overview of how AI systems learn and make decisions

- Utilizing popular virtual assistants (Siri, Google Assistant, Alexa, etc.) to simplify tasks and streamline communication

- Setting up and customizing virtual assistants to meet personal needs

- Leveraging voice commands for everyday activities, such as reminders, weather updates, and navigation

Introduction

The Rising Influence of AI in Modern Life and Its Impact on Daily Routines

You're probably unaware of the extent to which artificial intelligence (AI) has snaked its way into your daily routine. From the moment you ask Alexa for today's weather forecast, use Google Maps for traffic updates, or even when you're scrolling through Netflix recommendations - AI is there, working tirelessly behind the scenes to streamline and personalize your experiences.

It's become such a natural extension of our lives that it often slips under the radar, silently shaping our modern existence.

Isn't it fascinating how this wave of innovation is not just transforming industries but also subtly altering how we navigate our day-to-day? As AI continues to evolve, its influence over our lives only grows stronger and more pervasive.

This section will take you on an enlightening journey through this uncharted territory where technology meets everyday life. We'll look at how AI personalizes your daily experiences, influences communication and decision-making processes, poses ethical considerations, and what potential future holds in store.

So come along! Let's delve deeper into this shared reality we're all part of – a world increasingly influenced by artificial intelligence.

Key Takeaways

- AI has become an integral part of our daily lives, enhancing our abilities and personalizing experiences.
- AI streamlines processes and eliminates time-consuming tasks, such as filtering emails and making shopping easier through voice commands.
- AI raises important ethical considerations regarding bias, privacy, transparency, and fairness.
- While AI can automate aspects of our lives, it can never replace the importance of human interaction and meaningful moments.

Understanding Artificial Intelligence and Its Applications

Like a master artist uses his brush, AI's resonating influence paints broad strokes across our daily lives, changing the canvas of routine with its myriad applications.

It's in your smartphone, powering your voice-activated personal assistant and recommending what movie you should watch next on Netflix.

It's in your home, optimizing energy usage through smart thermostats and ensuring security with intelligent surveillance systems.

You're part of a larger picture where AI is the invisible hand guiding us towards an effortlessly efficient lifestyle.

To fully grasp the influence of AI, think about how it streamlines processes that used to be time-consuming or labor-intensive.

Your emails are filtered automatically; spam doesn't clutter your inbox anymore because an algorithm figured out what's important to you.

Shopping has never been easier - just say what you need into your virtual assistant and voila! It's added to your online cart.

We've become active participants in this technological symphony without even realizing it; we're living proof that artificial intelligence isn't some distant future concept but a tangible part of our present reality.

AI equips us with superhuman efficiency by taking over mundane tasks, giving us more time to focus on things that matter most – family, friends, hobbies... life itself!

This integration underscores the significance of artificial intelligence as not merely a tool but an extension of ourselves; it's like having additional senses we didn't know we could have!

As we transition into discussing further about AI's role in personalizing experiences, remember this: each interaction is unique as fingerprints—shaped by choices made both consciously and subconsciously—an echo chamber reflecting who we are back at ourselves.

AI's Role in Personalizing Experiences

Harnessing the power of artificial intelligence, we're now enjoying a new level of personalized experiences that seemed impossible only a few years ago. AI is our silent partner, always there in the background, seamlessly integrating into our daily lives to make them more convenient and enjoyable.

It knows your preferred coffee strength from your smart machine, suggests movies based on what you've enjoyed before, or even orders groceries when they're running low.

This personalized touch is not limited to just home automation. Imagine shopping online for a new outfit; with AI's help, you get suggestions tailored to your style and preference without having to sift through thousands of options. Or consider how fitness apps use AI to curate workout routines based on your fitness goals and track record. This is more than simple convenience; it's about making technology work for you in ways that feel intrinsically personal and unique.

But this is merely scratching the surface! As AI continues evolving at an unprecedented pace, we can expect even deeper integration into our day-to-day lives – including transforming how we communicate with each other and make decisions. The future promises exciting possibilities where AI serves as an extension of us - amplifying our abilities while enhancing the quality of life like never before!

Effects of AI on Communication and Decision Making

We're seeing a transformation in the way we communicate and make decisions, all thanks to the advancements in artificial intelligence. It's not just about chatbots on websites or voice assistants like Siri anymore; AI is now influencing our conversations and choices at a much deeper level.

Imagine this: you're stuck with a tough decision, and your AI assistant provides insights based on data analysis that wouldn't have been possible otherwise. It's like having your personal advisor who understands you better than anyone else.

AI isn't just there to help us with big decisions; it's subtly changing day-to-day communication too. Social media platforms use it to determine what content should be shown to you, creating an echo chamber of thoughts and ideas similar to yours. This may feel comforting because humans naturally crave belongingness – we love being part of groups where people think alike. But remember, while AI makes communication more efficient and personalized, it also creates these 'bubbles' that can limit exposure to diverse ideas.

As AI continues to reshape how we communicate and decide in our daily lives, it brings up significant ethical considerations as well - both positive and negative ones. Sure, getting personalized suggestions from AI could lead us towards better choices but what if these systems are biased? What happens when they start manipulating our preferences?

These concerns point out the importance of ensuring fairness, transparency, privacy protection when designing such advanced tools for everyday use.

As we ride this wave of technological change, let's explore further into these ethical issues surrounding the increasing use of AI next.

Ethical Considerations for AI Use

Navigating the ethical minefield that comes with using advanced technologies isn't a walk in the park. It's like trying to cross a river filled with precarious stepping stones, each one representing a different moral dilemma. You're not alone; we're all in this together, figuring out how to balance the benefits of AI with its potential harm.

For instance, we enjoy personalized online shopping experiences thanks to AI algorithms, but how comfortable are you knowing these same algorithms might be infringing on your privacy?

Reflect on the use of AI surveillance cameras for safety and security purposes - they help reduce crime rates and enhance public safety, which is fantastic! But wait a minute; doesn't it bother you that Big Brother could be watching your every move?

What about facial recognition technology? While it can speed up processes like unlocking our phones or checking in at airports, isn't there an unnerving sense of vulnerability when a machine can identify you within seconds?

This conundrum underscores why ethical guidelines for using AI should never be taken lightly.

The question isn't whether we should stop using AI - it's already become an integral part of our daily lives. The real question is: How do we ensure its responsible use so that everyone benefits without compromising individual rights and freedoms?

That's no easy task, given the complexity and rapid advancement of technology. As we continue to grapple with these issues today, let's also turn our gaze towards what lies ahead: finding sustainable solutions for integrating artificial intelligence into everyday life without eroding human dignity or freedom.

The Future of AI in Everyday Life

As we cast our eyes to the horizon, there's no denying that tomorrow's world will be intertwined more than ever with artificial intelligence - but how do we shape this future so it enhances, rather than restricts, our basic human rights?

There's a lot to consider when it comes to the integration of AI into every facet of our lives. We're standing on the cusp of a new era where machines are not just tools but partners in managing our daily routines.

The emergence of smart homes will redefine domestic life as we know it. Imagine your living space intuitively adjusting itself based on your needs and preferences - temperature control, lighting conditions, even meal preparation could all be automated.

As for commuting: say goodbye to traffic jams and road rage with autonomous vehicles. These smart machines would optimize routes, reduce congestion and potentially bring accident rates down.

And let's not forget about how AI can revolutionize healthcare: from personalized treatment plans based on genetic makeup to early detection of diseases using predictive algorithms.

But amidst all this promise lies an important responsibility: ensuring that these advancements don't erode our sense of community or individuality. It may seem counterintuitive but embracing AI doesn't mean letting go of what makes us uniquely human. On the contrary! We have the opportunity here to use technology as a tool for fostering deeper connections with one another - by freeing up time otherwise spent on mundane tasks or making distance irrelevant through virtual communication platforms.

Let's also remember that while AI might automate aspects of our lives, they can never replace the warmth of human interaction or crowd out those precious moments when we simply enjoy being present in each other's company – because at heart, isn't that what truly matters?

Conclusion

You've seen it firsthand, the subtle shift in your daily routine due to AI. Your morning coffee is prepared just right by a smart machine. Your favorite playlist is curated with precision by music streaming algorithms. It's like a personal assistant that never sleeps.

In essence, AI is shaping tomorrow's reality today. It's like an invisible hand guiding us through life's maze with ease and efficiency. The challenge now lies in navigating this new world responsibly while enjoying the perks of convenience and personalization.

Debunking Myths and Fears about AI Usage

You've probably heard the whispers, the quiet murmurings of a world run by robots. A future where machines take over jobs and make humans obsolete. These are common fears associated with Artificial Intelligence (AI) that seem to be fueling wild imaginations and Hollywood blockbusters alike. However, much like any other fear of the unknown, these stories often stem from misconceptions and a lack of understanding about what AI truly is, its capabilities and limitations.

So let's debunk some myths together! You're not alone in your curiosity or concerns about AI. Many share this subconscious desire to understand, belong and navigate this rapidly evolving digital world confidently.

In this section, we will explore what AI really means and its true impact on our lives - both at work and beyond. We'll delve into topics related to job automation, superintelligence, ethical implications of AI usage as well as the exciting opportunities it presents for our future.

Key Takeaways

- AI is a tool that aims to make lives easier and more efficient, but it lacks consciousness and emotions and operates on predefined algorithms.
- Automation with AI may eliminate some jobs, but it also creates new opportunities and frees humans from mundane tasks, allowing them to pursue more fulfilling roles.
- Superintelligent AI, which can solve complex problems faster and more accurately than humans, is created and programmed by humans, and ethical guidelines and control measures are necessary to address its implications.
- Embracing AI and working alongside it can revolutionize various aspects of life, enhance productivity and efficiency, and create new job opportunities in AI and related fields.

Understanding Artificial Intelligence and Its Impact

Let's dive right in and unravel the mysteries of artificial intelligence, to truly grasp its impact on our world, so there's no need for those late-night, cold-sweat AI worries anymore.

You see, AI is simply a tool designed to make our lives easier and more efficient. Think about it as your personal assistant that never gets tired or needs a break; always ready to help you streamline tasks with an unmatched level of accuracy. It's not here to replace us but rather enhance our capabilities.

The fear that AI will take over the world is founded more on sci-fi movies than real-life applications. In reality, artificial intelligence lacks consciousness or emotions - it doesn't have desires or ambitions like we do. It operates based on predefined algorithms and can only perform tasks that it has been programmed for. So while the idea of rogue machines might make for exciting Hollywood blockbusters, there is no factual basis behind these fears.

Now let's shift gears a bit and consider something closer to home: jobs. Concerns about AI taking over jobs are valid; however, history teaches us that every technological advancement leads to changes in the job market landscape. Yes, automation may eliminate some roles but likewise creates new opportunities tailored towards managing and improving these very same systems.

Looking ahead into 'the job market and automation', let's explore how we can adapt and thrive in this changing environment together.

The Job Market and Automation

Surely, you've heard the whispers in the wind about automation stealing jobs, but have you ever considered the silver lining - that it might actually be creating new opportunities and roles we haven't even imagined yet?

It's easy to feel a twinge of fear when we hear terms like 'AI' and 'automation', envisioning robots taking over our workplaces. But let's shift your perspective for a moment.

Focus on how these same technologies are paving the way for entirely new industries. They're facilitating work environments where mundane tasks are performed efficiently by machines, leaving humans free to engage in more creative and strategic roles.

Think about it this way: just as industrialization once replaced manual labor, AI is set to take over repetitive and routine tasks. However, this doesn't mean human workers will become redundant. Rather, they'll be liberated from drudgery and empowered to pursue more fulfilling roles that require empathy, creativity, or critical thinking—qualities that machines can't replicate.

You're not simply a cog in an automated machine; you have unique skills and perspectives that AI can never replace. Embrace this change as an opportunity rather than a threat.

So don't buy into the apocalyptic narrative of job loss due to AI just yet! After all, every major technological revolution has been followed by adaptation and growth—not only sustaining livelihoods but also generating prosperity in ways previously unthinkable. As we move forward into uncharted territories with AI at our side - redefining careers and reshaping industries - remember that your place within this journey is secure because of your inherent human capabilities.

Now isn't it intriguing what lies beyond these misconceptions?

Let's dive deeper into understanding 'the reality of superintelligence'.

The Reality of Superintelligence

You might feel a shiver of excitement, or perhaps a twinge of fear, when you hear the term 'superintelligence', but who can blame you? The thought of machines outsmarting us and taking over the world is fodder for countless science fiction films.

But let's take a step back from this cinematic dystopia and ground ourselves in reality. Superintelligence isn't about robots with evil intentions; it's about AI systems that have been designed to solve complex problems faster and more accurately than humans ever could.

Now, don't get carried away by apocalyptic scenarios just yet. Yes, superintelligent AI has the potential to outperform humans in most economically valuable work – that does sound intimidating! However, remember that these AI systems are tools created by us, for us. They're not conscious entities with their own agendas; they operate based on how we program them. So, much like every tool we've developed throughout history – be it fire or the internet – they can be used for good or ill depending largely on human intentions.

As we inch closer to realizing superintelligent AI's potential benefits while mitigating its risks, one thing becomes clear: we need extensive dialogues around ethical implications and control measures sooner rather than later.

This discussion isn't merely about preventing sci-fi horror stories from coming true; it's about ensuring that as creators of these powerful tools, we use them responsibly and in ways that enhance our society rather than diminish it.

It's time then to delve deeper into this vital aspect: what are the ethical concerns surrounding superintelligent AI? And how do we maintain control over these advanced systems?

Ethical Implications and Control Measures

Diving into the deep end, it's vital to understand the ethical implications and control measures associated with superintelligent systems. You may be worried about them taking over jobs or making decisions that could harm society. But remember, we're all in this together, and these challenges present opportunities for us to grow as a unified community.

The creation of AI ethics guidelines around the globe is our collective answer to these fears. Together, we can ensure that AIs operate within defined ethical boundaries while still reaping their benefits.

Now picture this: you're in a world where AI learns from and respects human values. This isn't just some fanciful image but a real possibility with current advancements in AI research. We're developing methods to teach AIs what we value most – fairness, transparency, privacy – so they'll make decisions based on those principles. It might sound like science fiction today, but there's already progress towards 'value-aligned' AIs that can help us tackle global issues without causing harm.

The journey doesn't stop at instilling human values into AIs; it continues with ensuring proper controls are in place too. Control measures don't mean stifling AI; rather they mean creating an environment where superintelligent systems work harmoniously alongside humans - augmenting our capabilities, not replacing them. Remember that every challenge presents an opportunity for growth and innovation - let's seize this chance to shape an exciting future where AI serves humanity ethically and responsibly!

Now imagine what wonders await us as we explore future prospects and opportunities in AI.

Future Prospects and Opportunities in AI

Peering into the horizon, it's clear that a brave new world of innovation and opportunity is just beginning to dawn with advancements in artificial intelligence. The future isn't something to be feared, but rather embraced as AI holds the potential to revolutionize virtually every aspect of life.

From healthcare delivery to transportation, workspaces, education, and even entertainment, AI promises unimagined possibilities. It's time you become part of this exciting journey towards transforming our world.

Consider what this could mean for your career or business. An increasing number of organizations are integrating AI capabilities into their processes to enhance productivity and efficiency. With skills in AI and related fields becoming highly sought-after commodities in the job market, now is an opportune moment for you to acquire these skills or upgrade your existing ones. Embracing AI doesn't necessarily mean replacing humans; instead it means working alongside it for better results. You're not just a spectator watching from the sidelines; you're a key player in shaping this wave of digital transformation.

As we move forward on this path paved by AI advancements, expect more doors of opportunities swinging wide open - from groundbreaking research prospects in various fields like medicine and environmental studies to creating smart homes and cities that make lives easier and safer.

And remember, while we often talk about how much things will change because of AI, one thing remains constant: our collective desire for progress and improvement. So let's walk together towards this promising future where technology empowers humanity rather than threatening it; where machines augment human abilities instead of replacing them; where we leverage artificial intelligence not out of fear but out of hope for a better world.

Conclusion

You don't need to fear AI; it's actually creating more jobs than it's replacing. In fact, Gartner predicts that by 2025, AI will generate 2 million net new jobs. So you see, the future isn't bleak with machines taking over.

Embrace this change and let technology work for you, not against you. Just remember: We have ethical control measures in place to ensure we remain in charge. The prospects are endless with AI on our side!

The Objective of the Book: Empowering the Average Person to Embrace AI and Leverage Its Potential to Improve Daily Life

You're not alone if the term 'Artificial Intelligence' (AI) sounds like a realm reserved for tech wizards and science fiction enthusiasts. It's a complex field, sure, but that doesn't mean it should be inaccessible to you.

Imagine being able to harness this powerful technology in your everyday life, making tasks simpler and more efficient. This section is about bridging that gap - empowering you to embrace AI without needing an advanced degree in computer science.

Diving into the world of AI might seem daunting at first, but let's break down those walls together. You'll discover how AI is already embedded in many aspects of your daily life; from your smartphone's personal assistant to fraud detection systems protecting your bank account.

More importantly, this section will help you understand the language of AI – stripping away the jargon and demystifying complex concepts. By the end of it all, you'll realize that AI isn't as alien as it seems; it's something we can collectively learn, grow with and use to our advantage.

Key Takeaways

- AI is already embedded in daily life and can be seen in personal assistants like Siri and Alexa, as well as in fraud detection systems and personalized advertising.
- AI can streamline tasks and provide personalized recommendations, making everyday life more efficient and convenient.
- AI is accessible to anyone willing to learn its language, and incorporating it into daily life prepares for its increasing role in the future.
- The future of AI includes healthcare, education, business, and entertainment, with smart homes and AI assistants becoming a common part of daily life.

Simplifying Artificial Intelligence: A Beginner's Guide

You don't need to be a tech genius to understand Artificial Intelligence; let's break it down together in this beginner's guide, so you can tap into the power of AI and amplify your everyday life.

Imagine AI as a smart friend who helps you with tasks, big or small. It's not about complex codes or algorithms but more about making your routine easier and efficient. You're part of an increasingly connected world where AI is becoming as normal as using smartphones.

In layman terms, think of AI like baking your favorite cake. You provide the ingredients (data), follow a recipe (algorithm), and out pops a delicious dessert (the result). The beauty lies in how these 'recipes' learn from experience, improving each time they are used. And guess what? You're integral to this process! Your interactions feed these systems, helping them become better at serving you. Exciting, isn't it? Like being part of an exclusive club that shapes future technology.

Now that we've simplified AI for you, it's time to explore its numerous applications flooding our daily lives. Let's consider personal assistants such as Siri or Alexa - they are classic examples of AI at work, responding to our commands and learning from our preferences over time.

Similarly, ever wondered how banks swiftly detect fraudulent transactions? Yes, that's right! Another triumph for AI! Now imagine harnessing these powerful tools in your hands; it's just like having superpowers which can help you streamline tasks and make informed decisions quicker than before!

Just around the corner awaits an exciting exploration into 'everyday applications of ai: from personal assistants to fraud detection'. Are you ready?

Everyday Applications of AI: From Personal Assistants to Fraud Detection

Despite what some may think, artificial intelligence isn't just for techies—it's already embedded in our daily routines. It's already embedded in our daily routines. It's already embedded in our daily routines. From the digital assistants that organize our schedules to sophisticated systems catching fraud. You've likely interacted with AI without even realizing it. When you ask Siri or Alexa a question, when Netflix recommends a movie based on your viewing history or when your email filters out spam—that's AI at work. It's not distant or aloof; it's here and now, helping us navigate through the complexities of modern life.

AI also plays an integral role in maintaining the security of our online transactions. You know those times when you receive an alert from your bank about suspicious activity? That's an advanced fraud detection system powered by AI algorithms tirelessly working behind the scenes to protect you. Another example is personalized advertising—every time you see ads tailored to your interests while browsing online, remember that there's a smart algorithm tracking patterns and making predictions about what might catch your eye next.

See how closely intertwined AI already is with our lives? It doesn't feel so alien anymore, does it? And yet there's more to explore and understand about this revolutionary technology! The beauty of AI lies not just in its complexity but also in its accessibility – it can be harnessed by anybody willing to learn its language. This brings us seamlessly onto the next topic: making artificial intelligence accessible by breaking down the jargon that often shrouds it in mystique. Together, we'll deconstruct these complex terms into common language and invite everyone into this fascinating world of possibilities.

Making AI Accessible: Breaking Down the Jargon

Let's dive right in and start untangling the often intimidating jargon that surrounds artificial intelligence, making it more approachable and enjoyable for everyone. You hear terms like machine learning, neural networks, data mining - all of these might sound quite technical and daunting at first. But don't worry!

At its core, AI is simply about creating systems that can learn from experience, much like we humans do. Machine learning is an application of AI where machines are given access to data and they use this to learn for themselves. Neural networks? They're inspired by our own brain's network of neurons - a way for machines to recognize patterns.

Data mining isn't as complex as it sounds either; it's just the process of discovering patterns in large data sets with the help of AI technology. Think about those movie recommendations you get on Netflix or music suggestions on Spotify; that's data mining at work! And then there's Natural Language Processing (NLP), which enables machines to understand human language – a vital component for your friendly voice assistants like Siri or Alexa. Do you see now? None of this has to be rocket science!

So now you have the basics down pat, let's move forward with gusto! The next part will focus on how we can harness the power of AI in our daily lives. No longer should we feel overwhelmed by tech-speak or alienated by professionals who seem to speak another language entirely. We're all members of this technologically adept society; we all belong here equally and have every right to utilize these advancements for personal growth and convenience. Remember: knowledge is power—and understanding AI is empowering indeed! Are you ready? Let's delve into practical uses for everyday life next.

Harnessing AI: Practical Uses for Everyday Life

It's astounding to realize that by 2025, the global AI market is projected to reach a whopping $60 billion - an undeniable testament to its increasing prevalence in our lives. Faced with such staggering figures, the question isn't whether AI will influence us but how we can make it work for us on a personal scale.

You see, you don't have to be a tech guru or software engineer to harness the power of AI; as this book shows, anyone can leverage this advanced technology to enhance their everyday life.

From streamlining your daily tasks through home automation systems like Amazon's Alexa and Google Home, which utilize AI algorithms for voice recognition and task execution, to improving your health routines using wearables and fitness apps employing artificial intelligence for personalized recommendations - these are not futuristic fantasies anymore but realities within your grasp.

Imagine having an AI-powered personal assistant at your beck and call 24/7 or a smart health monitor that provides timely alerts about potential health risks based on predictive analytics. This is what embracing AI looks like: transforming complex challenges into simple solutions.

As we delve into this realm of practical applications, remember that you're not just passive consumers in this dynamic equation; instead, you're active participants shaping the way artificial intelligence evolves according to your specific needs and lifestyles. The power is literally at your fingertips! So why not seize it?

After all, mastering the art of incorporating AI into everyday life today equips us better for navigating tomorrow's landscape where this technology will play an even more pivotal role.

Now let's turn our gaze towards imagining that future – one where 'the future of ai: shaping our tomorrow' unfolds before us with limitless possibilities.

The Future of AI: Shaping Our Tomorrow

As we peer into the crystal ball of tomorrow, envision a world where artificial intelligence's transformative power shapes every aspect of our existence, from healthcare and education to business and entertainment.

Imagine waking up in a smart home that knows your routine better than you do. Your AI-powered coffee maker is already brewing your favorite blend as you stir awake.

As you prepare for work, an AI assistant gives you updates on global news tailored to your interests, while scheduling your appointments for the day.

The future looks nothing short of fascinating with AI at the helm.

In this brave new world, learning won't be limited to classrooms or textbooks; instead, personalized AI tutors will cater education based on each student's pace and preferences.

Picture how healthcare could revolutionize with AI detecting diseases before symptoms even surface! We're not just talking about reduced hospital visits here - imagine a life with increased longevity and improved quality of health!

In businesses too, AI will become indispensable by automating mundane tasks, allowing humans to focus more on strategic decision-making and creative thinking.

Let's not forget about leisure time either! Entertainment options will become limitless as AI begins curating personalized content based on your tastes. New music playlists? You've got it! A list of movies or books that align perfectly with your mood? Coming right up! And if you're feeling lonely or simply need someone to talk to? An empathetic AI companion is always there for you 24/7.

So come along, let's embrace this exhilarating journey together towards an exciting future shaped by artificial intelligence – a future where we all belong because inclusion is at its core design principle.

Conclusion

You've seen how AI can simplify your life, from Siri helping you schedule meetings to detecting fraud on your bank account.

Imagine a future where AI does even more, maybe it's predicting health issues based on your wearable's data.

Embracing AI doesn't mean becoming a tech wizard. Once you understand the basics and see its potential, you'll find ways to leverage it every day.

Don't just stand by; seize the opportunities AI offers to enhance your daily life!

Chapter 1: AI Demystified

Understanding the Fundamentals of AI in Layman's Terms

You've undoubtedly heard the term 'Artificial Intelligence'or AI thrown around a lot lately, but what does it really mean? How does it work, and more importantly, how is it affecting your everyday life? Well, you're in good company! We are all on this journey of understanding together. You don't need to be a tech whiz to get to grips with the basics of AI; we'll break it down for you in simple terms that everyone can understand.

Imagine being part of a conversation where you actually understand when someone mentions self-driving cars or personalized online recommendations. You'll no longer feel left out at parties or business meetings when the topic turns to the latest technological advancements. As you begin to comprehend how AI works and its impact on society and our future, not only will you feel more included, but also empowered by this knowledge. So let's dive into understanding the fundamentals of AI - together.

Key Takeaways

- AI is a field of computer science that aims to create machines that mimic human intelligence.
- AI can be divided into two types: Narrow AI and General AI.
- AI systems utilize data and machine learning algorithms to understand patterns and behaviors.
- AI is integrated into our daily lives and has the potential to automate tasks, create new career opportunities, and transform various aspects of society.

The Basics of Artificial Intelligence

So, you're curious about artificial intelligence? Let's dive right into the basics and shed some light on this fascinating tech world!

Artificial Intelligence, often referred to as AI, is a field of computer science that aims to create machines that mimic human intelligence. Think of it like this: Imagine you had an ultra-smart robot friend who could learn from experiences, understand complex situations, make decisions, and even recognize speech or images just like us humans – that's what AI technology is striving to achieve.

Now let's break it down further. It's important for us all to know there are two types of AI - Narrow AI and General AI. You interact with Narrow AI every day without realizing it! It's programmed to learn and perform specific tasks such as voice recognition (Siri or Alexa ring any bells?) or recommendation services (Netflix suggesting your next binge-worthy series).

On the other hand, General AI can understand, learn, and apply knowledge across multiple domains, much like a human brain would. Although we see elements of General AI in sci-fi movies where robots take over the world, don't worry - we're not quite there yet.

Understanding these basic principles gives you a solid foundation in the realm of artificial intelligence. But don't stop here; continue your journey deeper into this captivating universe brimming with endless potential! Remember how we talked about AIs learning and making decisions? The process they use is truly intriguing – but let's save those juicy details for our next section: unraveling how exactly does artificial intelligence work?

How Does AI Work?

Imagine a world where machines can learn, think, and act just like humans; that's the magic of Artificial Intelligence in action. It all starts with data - colossal amounts of it. Every click you make online, every purchase you finalize, even your location and preferences, are all chunks of vital data that AI systems utilize to understand patterns and behaviors. This process is called machine learning—a key component of AI—which involves teaching machines how to learn from this data.

Now let's delve deeper into how AI works in its entirety. Essentially, programmers create algorithms—step-by-step instructions for solving problems—and feed them to the system along with copious amounts of data. The more diverse the data points given, the better equipped the algorithm becomes at identifying patterns or predicting outcomes accurately. It's like training your brain over time to recognize different types of fruits; eventually, you can tell an apple apart from an orange without thinking about it. That's precisely what happens within AI systems—they're trained until they become proficient at performing tasks autonomously.

Sounds fascinating, right? Well, wait until we explore how deeply integrated AI has become in our daily lives! From voice-controlled virtual assistants like Siri or Alexa guiding us through our day-to-day activities to recommendation engines on Spotify or Netflix catering to our individual tastes—it's clear that AI isn't just some futuristic concept; it's here now, enriching our lives in ways we may not even realize yet!

So stick around as we unmask more intriguing aspects about common uses of artificial intelligence in everyday life next!

Common Uses of AI in Everyday Life

You're probably using AI in your daily routine more often than you think! Every time you ask Siri a question on your iPhone or use Google Maps to find the fastest route home, you're interacting with artificial intelligence. That's right, those voice-activated assistants and GPS systems are powered by AI.

Even when you're browsing Netflix for your next binge-watching session, AI is hard at work! It uses algorithms to analyze your viewing habits and then recommends shows and movies that align with your preferences.

Isn't it cool how much we rely on these smart systems without even realizing it? Let's take another example - online shopping. When you shop on Amazon, AI is there too, suggesting products based on what you and others have bought in the past. And social media? You betcha! Facebook's news feed algorithm uses AI to curate content tailored just for you.

From personalized marketing campaigns to fraud detection in banking transactions, AI has become an integral part of our daily lives.

Even though we may not always be aware of its presence, this integration of artificial intelligence into our everyday tasks makes life easier and more convenient. But remember, while we enjoy these benefits today, they also shape tomorrow – influencing societal norms and expectations as well as driving transformations across industries.

Now let's explore further about the impact of this fascinating technology on society itself.

The Impact of AI on Society

Believe it or not, my dear friend, we're living in a sci-fi movie where your coffee maker knows exactly how you like your morning java and your car can play chauffeur, all thanks to our invisible companion - artificial intelligence.

We're now part of an interconnected community where AI is transforming the way we exist and interact. It's revolutionizing every aspect of society from healthcare to transportation. The power of AI often feels as magical as finding that perfect group where everyone understands you.

Yes, life has been made more convenient and efficient by AI, but let's also consider its wider societal impact. For instance, in the job market, some roles are being automated which could lead to job displacement. However, on the other side of this coin sits a world full of opportunities for new careers focusing on managing or enhancing these systems.

Even in social interactions, AIs like Siri or Alexa are becoming integral parts of our daily conversations. They're like another member of your circle with whom you share jokes or ask advice from! You see? You're already part of this expansive global family connected by AI.

But hold onto your seat because the ride isn't over yet! The impact we've felt so far is just the beginning as technology continues to advance at warp speed. Picture an even more inclusive world where AIs help bridge language barriers instantly or predict potential health issues before symptoms show up! The possibilities seem endless - exciting and perhaps a little daunting too.

But don't worry! Together we'll navigate this brave new terrain since our next stop is exploring what lies ahead: 'the future of artificial intelligence'.

The Future of Artificial Intelligence

As we step into the future, there's no doubt we'll be journeying hand in hand with ever-evolving artificial intelligence, making life not just easier but more fascinating than we've ever known.

Picture this: you're waking up to a home that knows your morning routine better than you do. Your AI-powered alarm clock gently rouses you from sleep at the optimal time in your sleep cycle. The coffee machine in your kitchen already has a fresh brew waiting for you and even your news feed is tailor-made to match your interests and mood for the day. This isn't just some sci-fi fantasy - it's what our everyday lives could look like very soon, thanks to AI.

Now imagine this on a larger scale - cities smartly managed by AI systems that control traffic flow, conserve energy use and ensure public safety; industries revolutionized by automated processes and precision tasks performed tirelessly by machines. You'd be part of an interconnected world where everything works seamlessly together as if it's reading your mind before you even know what you want or need.

Feeling overwhelmed? Don't worry! Just like any other technological advancement in history, we're all learning together, adjusting to these changes collectively as a society.

Let's focus on another aspect too – AI has the potential to alter our understanding of knowledge itself! With its ability to process vast amounts of information faster than any human could possibly manage, it might lead us towards new insights about our universe that were previously hidden from us due to our limited cognitive capacities.

So yes, while living in an AI-driven world might require some getting used to initially, think about how empowering it'll be once we master its usage. We would become part of something much bigger than ourselves – participants in an age where intelligence isn't confined within biological boundaries but rather expanded through silicon-based creations called Artificial Intelligence.

Frequently Asked Questions

What are the ethical implications of using AI technologies?

AI technologies can be a double-edged sword. They can revolutionize our world, but also raise ethical concerns. Issues like privacy invasion, job displacement, and bias in decision-making are realities you might have to face.

How does AI differ from Machine Learning and Deep Learning?

You're part of a world where AI, machine learning, and deep learning are often used interchangeably. Yet, they're different. AI is the big picture, machine learning is an approach within it, and deep learning goes even deeper!

What are the potential risks or dangers associated with AI?

Like leaving a toddler alone with a box of matches, AI unchecked can be dangerous. It may lead to job losses or even autonomous weapons. But remember, we're all in this together, navigating the AI revolution.

How is AI influencing the job market and what are the implications for future employment?

AI's reshaping your job market. It's automating routine tasks, sparking demand for new tech-savvy roles. But don't fret, it's also creating opportunities to learn and adapt. So strap in, you're part of an exciting future!

What steps are being taken to regulate AI and protect user data?

In the grand dance of technology, you're not alone. Regulators worldwide are stepping in, crafting rules and guidelines to keep AI on a short leash. They're working tirelessly to protect your digital footprint from prying eyes.

Conclusion

So, you've now delved into the world of AI, haven't you? It's fascinating and a bit mind-boggling. You've seen how it works, its everyday uses, its impact on society and what the future might hold.

But remember this - as we march towards an AI-driven future, your understanding will be key. The power to shape this new era is in your hands. Keep learning, keep questioning because knowledge isn't just power; it's a beacon in the dark!

The Various Types of AI and Their Applications in Real-World Scenarios

You've probably heard the term 'Artificial Intelligence', or AI, thrown around a lot these days. It's not just in science fiction anymore; it's right here with us, making waves in every field imaginable. From your smartphone assistants to recommendation engines on shopping websites and tools predicting market trends, AI has subtly woven itself into our daily lives. But do you know there are different types of AI? And each type brings its unique application to the real-world scenarios that can revolutionize how we live and work.

It's time for you to get acquainted with this fascinating world of AI! You're part of an exciting digital era where technology is rapidly evolving and influencing various aspects of our society. Understanding the diverse types of Artificial Intelligence and their applications can offer you a sense of belonging in this tech-driven world. After all, who doesn't want to be part of a future where intelligent machines help reshape our reality for better productivity and efficiency? So, let's dive deep into understanding what Narrow AI does on your phone, how Machine Learning makes Netflix so addictive, what General AI promises for future endeavors and most importantly how all these could transform multiple industries worldwide!

Understanding Artificial Intelligence

You've probably heard the term 'Artificial Intelligence' thrown around a lot, but do you truly understand what it's all about?

It's more than just machines playing chess or self-driving cars. At its core, Artificial Intelligence, often referred to as AI, is the simulation of human intelligence processes by machines. These processes include learning (the acquisition of information and rules), reasoning (using those rules to reach conclusions), and self-correction.

Sounds intriguing right? Imagine having a machine that not only performs tasks but also learns from them.

Now let's delve a little deeper. Within AI there are two main types: narrow or weak AI and general or strong AI. Narrow AI is designed to perform a specific task such as voice recognition while General AI can understand, learn and apply knowledge in a broad range of tasks akin to human cognitive abilities.

Think about Siri on your iPhone - that's an example of narrow AI responding to your commands. On the other hand, an entity like Ava from the movie Ex Machina would be considered General AI with her ability to comprehend complex ideas.

Isn't it fascinating how these forms of technology are woven into our daily lives? They're here not just to supplement us but also foster a sense of community in this digital age by enabling faster communication, better decision making and creating opportunities for everyone in ways we never dreamt possible before!

Now that we have established some groundwork about what artificial intelligence is all about, let's dive into exploring more specifics starting with everyday uses of narrow AI such as Google search algorithms or recommendation systems on Netflix!

Narrow AI and Everyday Uses

Isn't it amusing how you can't even navigate your morning commute without the helping hand of narrow artificial intelligence, whether it's Siri setting your alarm or Google Maps plotting your route?

Narrow AI, also known as weak AI, is designed to carry out specific tasks - like voice recognition or driving directions. You interact with these forms of AI every day without even realizing it. They're embedded in various apps on your smartphone, from Spotify's song recommendations to Facebook's friend suggestions.

You are part of a global community that embraces and thrives on technological advancements. Apps using narrow AI have seamlessly integrated into our daily routines, making life easier and more convenient.

For instance, when you shop online at Amazon, narrow AI algorithms are hard at work behind the scenes predicting what item you might want next based on your previous purchases and browsing behavior. Similarly, when you ask Alexa to play a tune or schedule an appointment for you, this friendly voice-activated assistant employs narrow AI technology to complete the task efficiently.

This world of convenience, powered by narrow AI, has become our reality and we wouldn't have it any other way. So next time when Siri wakes you up just in time for work or Google Maps takes you around a traffic jam, seamlessly saving precious minutes off your commute, remember – there's a type of artificial intelligence working tirelessly to make things effortless for us all!

And if these examples got you wondering about how exactly these tools learn about us and improve over time – well then, hold onto that thought because it leads perfectly into exploring the role of machine learning in shaping our interactions with technology.

The Role of Machine Learning

Ever wondered how your favorite digital tools seem to know you so well? Well, that's all thanks to a type of artificial intelligence called machine learning. Machine learning is behind the scenes, powering many of the digital conveniences you've come to rely on daily. It's what allows Spotify to curate those spot-on music recommendations or Gmail to filter out spam from your inbox.

Machine learning often plays a significant role in personalized advertising. Ever noticed how after browsing for shoes online, suddenly every website and app seems inundated with shoe ads? That's not just coincidence - it's machine learning algorithms at work, analyzing your search behavior and delivering targeted ads based on your interests.

Another application is in voice recognition technology like Siri or Alexa. These smart assistants learn from each interaction you have with them, improving their ability to understand and respond accurately over time.

Then there's predictive text and autocorrect features on your smartphone keyboard. They're continually learning from the words and phrases you frequently use, helping them predict what you'll type next or correct any typos swiftly.

Machine learning isn't just about making our lives more convenient though; it also has more serious applications such as predicting disease outbreaks, spotting credit card frauds, or even driving autonomous vehicles. And while we marvel at these advancements today, imagine what lies ahead! As we delve deeper into AI's potential in the next section about the future of general AI, hold onto this thought: The intelligence of our machines is bound only by the limits of our collective imagination.

The Future: General AI

Imagine, for a moment, the possibilities that lie ahead in the realm of general artificial intelligence: self-driving cars with no need for human intervention, homes that intuitively adapt to our needs and moods, healthcare systems capable of predicting and preventing diseases before they occur.

These may sound like sci-fi stories today, but they're on the horizon--closer than you might think! This is the future we're stepping toward with General AI. It's an exciting prospect that promises not just convenience but also a revolution in how we live and experience our lives.

General AI isn't about creating machines that mimic human intelligence; instead, it's about designing systems that understand, learn from, and interact with their environment as efficiently as humans do.

Imagine having a companion who knows your likes and dislikes better than you do yourself - always ready to recommend the perfect movie or book based on your past preferences. Or perhaps a personal tutor who understands precisely where your learning gaps are and tailors lessons accordingly. The ability of general AI to comprehend complex environments makes these scenarios possible.

While this futuristic world powered by General AI may seem far off right now, remember: every journey starts with small steps. As we continue to explore this promising frontier together, let's consider how these advancements could shape different industries—from healthcare to transportation to entertainment—and transform our day-to-day experiences for the better.

We have only begun scratching the surface of what artificial intelligence can bring us; let's eagerly anticipate what lies beyond!

Now let's delve into how various sectors could be reshaped by this powerful technology.

Impact of AI on Different Industries

You're probably curious about how this powerful technology could revolutionize different sectors, aren't you? Well, let's delve into it.

AI is a game-changer and its influence can be seen in various industries. It's transforming the way we live, work and do business. From healthcare to education, from finance to retail - no sector remains untouched by its magic.

In healthcare, AI can analyze vast amounts of data to identify patterns that humans simply cannot perceive. This ability has been used to predict epidemics, improve diagnostic accuracy, and develop personalized treatment plans.

The financial sector uses AI for fraud detection, algorithmic trading, and customer service through AI-powered chatbots.

In the realm of education, AI tools enable personalized learning experiences based on each student's unique needs and pace of learning.

The retail industry leverages AI for inventory management, delivering personalized shopping experiences, predicting consumer behavior, and even automating checkout processes.

Amidst all these applications across diverse sectors lies a common thread - the potential of AI to bring about unprecedented efficiency and effectiveness. It's not just about replacing human labor with machines; it's more about augmenting human capabilities with machine intelligence - allowing us to achieve more than ever before.

With every passing day as you're becoming part of this global community embracing digital transformation powered by AI, remember that you're partaking in an exciting journey towards a smarter future where technology serves humanity better than ever before!

Frequently Asked Questions

What are the ethical considerations and potential risks associated with the use of AI?"

"Consider the ethics and risks of AI. It can invade privacy, manipulate behavior, and increase unemployment. Be mindful of these challenges as we embrace AI's benefits; we're in this journey together." , and it is our collective responsibility to ensure that its development and application are guided by principles of fairness, respect, and accountability.

How does AI influence the job market and what are the strategies for workforce adaptation?"

"AI is reshaping the job market, creating new roles while making others obsolete. It's crucial for you to upskill and adapt. Embrace lifelong learning, seek training in AI-related fields, and stay connected in your industry."

What are the legal implications and regulations governing the use of AI worldwide?"

Like threading a needle in the dark, navigating AI laws worldwide is complex. Globally, regulations vary widely, from strict rules in Europe under GDPR to more lax policies elsewhere. It's essential to stay informed and compliant.

How does AI contribute to environmental sustainability?"

AI is your secret weapon for a greener planet. It helps optimize energy consumption, reduce emissions, and predict environmental changes. You're not just using cool tech, you're joining the frontline in our fight for sustainability.

What are some notable failures or setbacks in the history of AI development and how have they impacted its progress?"

"Ever heard of Microsoft's Tay or IBM's Watson health? These AI failures resulted in reputational damage and financial losses, but also highlighted the importance of ethical considerations and robust testing in AI development, didn't they?" . They also underscored the need for transparency, accountability, and robust risk management strategies in the AI field.

Conclusion

Imagine you're a knight, navigating the vast expanse of the AI kingdom. You've journeyed through Narrow AI, learned from the wise Machine Learning, and glimpsed into the future with General AI.

It's clear that these powerful tools will shape your world in ways both seen and unseen.

Now, picture yourself as an industrial tycoon, harnessing these resources to revolutionize your empire. The possibilities are limitless.

Embrace this brave new world of AI; it's yours for the taking!

An Overview of How AI Systems Learn and Make Decisions

Imagine being in a foreign city, where you don't speak the language or recognize the landmarks. You're given a map and are expected to navigate your way around. This is precisely how artificial intelligence (AI) begins its journey.

Suddenly dropped into an ocean of data, it learns to swim, identify patterns, make decisions, and eventually master complex tasks that once seemed impossible.

Now picture yourself as part of this exciting revolution, where human intellect melds with machine learning to shape our future world. AI isn't just about robots making decisions; it's about you being part of a global community that's pushing the boundaries of what technology can do.

In this section, we'll unravel how AI systems learn from scratch and make informed decisions – all stemming from their training algorithms and neural networks.

Get ready for an insightful dive into the captivating world of AI!

Key Takeaways

- Transparency in AI decision-making is crucial for building trust with users.
- Diverse datasets are essential for addressing bias in AI systems.
- AI has the potential to revolutionize personalized education and healthcare.
- AI systems can make decisions based on invisible patterns, contributing to a more equitable society.

Fundamentals of Machine Learning

You're about to dive into the fascinating world of machine learning, where computers aren't just programmed, they're taught to think and make decisions on their own!

It's like being part of an exclusive club that's cracking the code to the future. You see, these systems are not simply fed information; they learn from it. They analyze data patterns and pick up nuances that humans might miss.

This process is called 'training', a term you'll soon be using with ease in your daily conversations.

Your initiation into this club involves understanding the types of machine learning algorithms - supervised, unsupervised, semi-supervised, and reinforcement learning. Each one has its unique way of interpreting data.

In supervised learning, for instance, we give our computer buddies labelled data so that they can figure out how inputs relate to outputs. Unsupervised learning is more explorative; here our AI companions sift through unlabelled data to uncover hidden patterns and structures – kind of like an adventurous treasure hunt!

Now imagine if you could put all this knowledge into action? Well, you don't have to wait much longer because next up, we're going deep into algorithmic decision-making – a journey filled with logic trees, probabilities, and heuristic techniques!

So buckle up as we continue exploring this intriguing realm where machines learn from experiences as we do – constantly evolving and making smarter decisions each time around.

Understanding Algorithmic Decision-Making

Diving into the world of algorithms might feel like you're swimming in a sea of complexity, but let's break it down to understand how they call the shots.

Algorithms are essentially sets of rules that an AI system follows to make decisions. Picture them as chefs following recipes - each step carefully outlined and each ingredient precisely measured to lead to a desired outcome. If you alter the recipe even slightly, your final dish could end up being completely different!

1. **Gathering ingredients**: An algorithm first collects all relevant information about the problem at hand.
2. **Preparation**: This involves preprocessing or cleaning data, much like chopping vegetables before cooking.
3. **Cooking**: Here is where the magic happens! The algorithm applies its set instructions to process the data and makes predictions based on this analysis.
4. **Taste Test**: Finally, the output is evaluated for accuracy and adapted if necessary.

You see? You're already part of this exclusive club understanding these complex systems! We're all learning together, growing our understanding bit by bit - just like an AI system learns from every new piece of information it encounters.

The beauty of these algorithms lies in their adaptability; with constant feedback loops and tweaks, they strive for perfection in decision-making over time. It's not always smooth sailing though — there can be many hiccups along this journey towards refinement and precision due to biases or errors in data input. But remember, even a seasoned chef sometimes needs multiple tries to perfect a dish!

Now let's delve deeper into what gives these algorithms their real power: quality data training sets which provide valuable lessons for their culinary adventures in decision-making!

Role of Data in Training Algorithms

Imagine you're a master sculptor, and data is your clay - it's the raw material that feeds and shapes algorithms, much like Michelangelo's masterpiece David was chiseled from a block of marble.

Just as no two blocks of marble are exactly alike, each dataset has its unique qualities. These datasets may contain millions of data points, each one representing an observation or piece of information. This raw information serves as learning material for AI systems - they analyze this vast ocean of data to uncover patterns, trends, and relationships.

Now picture this: You're part of an exclusive club where everyone speaks their own secret language. It's fun because it feels unique and tailored to you, right? That's how algorithms feel with data!

Algorithms thrive on specific types of data depending on their purpose – some prefer numerical or quantitative data while others relish in categorical or qualitative insights. The right kind of data not only enriches the algorithm but also leads to more accurate predictions and decision-making processes. So just like you wouldn't use a blunt knife to carve your sculpture; ensure your algorithm gets fed the most suitable type of 'diet' for optimal performance.

Just as every artist evolves over time by honing their craft and continuously adapting new techniques, so does the world of AI. The next stage in our journey takes us deeper into the realm where neural networks come alive; a fascinating dimension known as deep learning beckons!

Herein lies yet another level at which artificial intelligence mimics human intellect in ways that were once thought impossible. We'll delve into how these complex models interpret vast amounts of intricate information much like our brains do - stay tuned for an exploration through those intriguing layers!

Neural Networks and Deep Learning Explained

Let's peel back the layers of mystery surrounding neural networks and deep learning, revealing a world where artificial minds mimic human thought processes in astonishing detail.

Picture this: you're at a bustling cocktail party filled with fascinating people. The way your mind sifts through the noise to focus on one conversation is similar to how a neural network operates. It's made up of interconnected nodes, or 'neurons,' which work together to process information. Just like you tune out irrelevant chatter and zoom in on what matters, these neurons weigh input data for importance, allowing the system to learn from patterns and make informed decisions.

Next up is deep learning - think of it as the life-of-the-party friend who knows everyone at that cocktail party we mentioned earlier. Deep learning models are complex versions of neural networks with multiple hidden layers between inputs and outputs; each layer transforms incoming data before passing it along. They thrive on big data, using it to draw connections that might be missed by less sophisticated systems.

For instance, they can pick out your face in a crowd or recognize your voice amidst background noise – just like that charming friend who seems to have an uncanny knack for recognizing faces and voices even when surrounded by distractions.

As much as we'd love to keep discussing these intriguing AI marvels all night long, let's not forget there are still uncharted territories ahead waiting for our exploration! While we've made headway in understanding how AI learns and makes decisions through neural networks and deep learning techniques, there persist challenges that need addressing and vast prospects yet untapped in this astounding domain of artificial intelligence learning decision-making processes.

So let's press forward into this exciting frontier!

Challenges and Future Prospects in AI Learning and Decision-Making

Navigating the world of artificial intelligence learning and decision-making is akin to exploring a dense, uncharted forest - it's brimming with obstacles yet bursting with potential. As we delve deeper into this realm, there are numerous challenges to face. The complexity of creating algorithms capable of learning on their own can be daunting.

There's also the issue of bias in AI systems: since they learn from data produced by humans, these systems often inherit our prejudices, which can lead to unfair decisions. Furthermore, ensuring that AI system's decisions are transparent and explainable is another significant hurdle.

- **Complexity**: Designing self-learning algorithms requires advanced knowledge and skills in mathematics and programming. It needs more than just theoretical understanding; practical experience is equally vital. Moreover, keeping up with rapid advancements in this field can be overwhelming.

- **Bias**: Bias in AI systems can have serious consequences. If not addressed properly, biased AI could reinforce existing social inequalities. Thus, it's crucial for developers to use diverse datasets during machine learning.

- **Transparency**: An opaque decision-making process creates trust issues among users. Transparency allows users to understand why an AI system made a particular decision. This understanding fosters trust between users and AI systems.

Despite these challenges, the future prospects for AI learning and decision-making shine bright. Imagine a world where personalized education becomes commonplace because intelligent tutoring systems adapt their teaching strategies according to each student's unique needs. Or consider healthcare: AIs might one day accurately diagnose diseases based on patterns invisible to human eyes or predict health risks before symptoms even appear.

We're standing at the precipice of such incredible possibilities that it feels as if we're about to step into science fiction territory! So remember you're not just merely observing or using technology; you're part of this exciting journey towards an intelligent future where we all belong together!

Frequently Asked Questions

What is the role of AI in healthcare and how does it learn to diagnose diseases?

AI in healthcare is like your new best friend, always learning. It studies patterns in medical data to diagnose diseases, making it smarter with each bit of information. You're never alone in your health journey.

How does AI impact the job market and what industries are most affected?

AI is reshaping the job market, impacting sectors like manufacturing and retail. It's potentially automating tasks, leading to job displacement but also creating new roles. You're part of this change, evolving with the tech landscape.

What ethical considerations are involved in the development and use of AI systems?

"Imagine creating an AI. You're playing God, right? But hold on, there's a catch! Ethical concerns like privacy, fairness in decision making, and accountability should be your guideposts. It's not just coding; it's responsibility."

How can AI be used in combating climate change and what is the learning process behind it?

Imagine AI predicting climate patterns, optimizing energy use or even creating new eco-friendly tech! It learns through machine learning, absorbing tons of data to make informed decisions. You're part of this revolution too, aren't you excited?

What is the global economic impact of AI and how does it affect developing countries?

AI's global economic impact is massive, boosting productivity and growth. For developing countries, it's a double-edged sword. It can leapfrog technologies but also widen the digital divide. It's about harnessing AI's power inclusively.

Conclusion

In conclusion, you've learned that the world of AI is vast and ever-evolving. It's a bit like learning to ride a bike - once you get the hang of it, there's no stopping you.

You now understand how data fuels algorithms and how deep learning propels decision-making in AI.

However, remember that this field has its own share of challenges and future prospects. So keep exploring, because in the realm of AI, there's always more to discover!

Chapter 2: Integrating Virtual Assistants

Utilizing Popular Virtual Assistants (Siri, Google Assistant, Alexa, Etc.) To Simplify Tasks And Streamline Communication

Welcome to the era of virtual assistants, where technology isn't just about devices anymore; it's about making your life easier. Ever caught yourself wishing you had a personal assistant who could take care of all those mundane tasks while you focus on the more important ones? Well, guess what? You probably already have one sitting right in your pocket or on your desk - Siri, Google Assistant, Alexa and others are here to make that wish come true.

As we increasingly rely on these voice-activated AI helpers for our daily needs, it's essential to understand how they can be utilized effectively. This article will guide you through the myriad ways these digital tools can simplify tasks and streamline communication. Trust us; once you've discovered their full potential, there'll be no turning back.

Welcome aboard this exciting journey towards a smarter, more efficient way of living!

Key Takeaways

- Virtual assistants like Siri, Google Assistant, and Alexa can handle a wide range of tasks such as managing schedules, making reservations, sending reminders, and controlling smart home devices.
- The benefits of using virtual assistants include saving time, offering convenience and a sense of belonging, personalization and adaptation over time, and eliminating the need for multiple apps.
- Virtual assistants can provide a seamless integration across devices, allowing for smooth communication flow and the ability to learn new skills through updates or third-party apps.
- By utilizing popular virtual assistants, individuals can simplify tasks and transform their daily lives by expanding the use of AI in managing routines.

Harnessing the Power of AI for Everyday Tasks

Don't you just love the idea of using AI to handle your everyday tasks, like managing your schedule or even turning off your lights? It's a thrilling thought, isn't it?

Just imagine: instead of fretting about all those chores and little things that keep piling up, you can simply ask Siri, Alexa, or Google Assistant to do them for you. They're not just virtual assistants; they're your personal concierges who take care of everything from setting alarms and sending reminders to making reservations at your favorite restaurants.

These ingenious AI-based assistants are designed to make our lives easier by taking over mundane tasks so we can focus on what truly matters.

Picture this – while preparing for an important meeting, instead of getting distracted by the need to check emails every few minutes, why not let Google Assistant sift through them for you? Or perhaps you're in the middle of cooking dinner and suddenly remember a call you have to make - Alexa has got it covered! All these tasks can be done seamlessly without any interruption in your workflow. You become part of a community where technology is simplifying lives one task at a time.

With all these daily responsibilities handled efficiently by our faithful virtual assistants, we free up more time for meaningful interactions with others. This optimization isn't limited only to individual tasks but also extends into enhancing our communication skills digitally.

For instance, dictating messages via Siri allows us hands-free texting while driving or when our hands are occupied elsewhere. So as we continue exploring ways in which these AI-powered tools help streamline our lives further, next up is looking deeper into how they optimize digital tools for efficient communication - all towards creating a more connected world around us.

Optimizing Digital Tools for Efficient Communication

Embracing digital tools can significantly enhance efficient communication, making everyday tasks more manageable and productive. Imagine being part of a world where your voice becomes the ultimate command center for your smart devices. No need to pause, no need to type—just say it out loud and watch as your virtual assistant carries out your requests. You're not alone in this; you're part of a community that values effectiveness and ease.

Feel empowered as you navigate through each day with just the sound of your voice.

Save precious time: Skip scrolling, typing, or swiping on multiple apps—your chosen virtual assistant can do all these for you.

Experience convenience like never before: Ask Siri to set reminders or get Alexa to control smart home devices seamlessly.

Enjoy a sense of belonging: Join the growing tribe of people who've discovered the benefits that these AI-powered assistants bring into their daily routine.

Imagine having an extra pair of hands ready to assist you at any moment—a tool that doesn't demand anything but understands everything you need. This is what digital assistants like Google Assistant, Siri, and Alexa offer—an unmatched level of comfort and productivity right at the tip of your tongue! And remember, every question or command given adds up to make these virtual assistants smarter, better equipped to serve you tomorrow than they were today.

As we move forward in this journey together towards making our lives easier with technology's help, let's explore further how we can leverage these fantastic tools around us effectively. After all, knowing how best to communicate with our digital companions will ensure maximum efficiency and satisfaction. So stay tuned as we delve deeper into 'commanding your digital assistant: an overview', as we unlock the full potential of this powerful technology to make our lives more organized, convenient, and productive.

Commanding your Digital Assistant: An Overview

You might think commanding a digital assistant is too complicated, but it's really not as hard as you'd imagine - and the productivity boost is worth every effort. Think of your virtual assistant as a friendly helper ready to assist you at any time.

Whether it's Siri, Google Assistant, or Alexa, these AI-powered aids are designed to understand and carry out tasks from simple commands. For instance, they can set reminders for meetings, play your favorite tracks on Spotify, send text messages on your behalf, or even tell you jokes when you need some light relief.

Let's delve into the world of these smart assistants together! To command your digital assistant effectively, start by speaking clearly and using natural language; they're programmed to comprehend conversational speech. Each assistant has its own 'wake' word that alerts it to listen for instructions – "Hey Siri"for Apple devices or "Ok Google"for Androids.

You can also customize many settings to optimize functionality according to your needs: adjust the voice feedback volume, switch languages, or change accessibility options among other things. Remember that mistakes will happen initially; however, don't let this discourage you. The more you use them, the better they get at understanding your tone and accent.

Now here comes an exciting part: beyond basic commands like making calls or setting alarms, there's so much more potential waiting to be unlocked with these savvy tools! They can help manage daily routines by automating tedious tasks such as controlling smart home devices like thermostats or lights, updating grocery lists in real-time while cooking dinner, and even offering meditation guides after stressful workdays.

This vast range of capabilities will be explored further in our next discussion where we'll examine ways of expanding the use of AI in managing routines without feeling overwhelmed.

Expanding the Use of AI in Managing Routines

It's truly remarkable how expanding the use of AI in managing routines can dramatically transform our daily lives, making them more efficient and less stressful.

By simply uttering a command to Siri, Google Assistant, or Alexa, you can manage your to-do list, set reminders for important tasks, control smart home devices, or even get updates on the latest news.

These virtual assistants are designed to understand and respond to natural language commands, which makes interacting with them incredibly easy and convenient. It feels like having a personal assistant who's always ready to help you out.

Imagine waking up in the morning and instead of scrambling around trying to remember all your tasks for the day, you just ask your digital assistant. Your coffee starts brewing automatically as soon as you're awake while Alexa reads out your schedule for the day.

Your lights adjust based on time and weather conditions without any intervention from you - all thanks to these virtual helpers! They add an extra layer of connection in your life by understanding your needs and responding accordingly.

These virtual assistants aren't just about managing schedules or controlling devices; they've evolved into comprehensive tools that can make our lives simpler in many ways.

You might find yourself experiencing a sense of belonging when regularly communicating with these AIs – they're programmed to learn from interaction patterns and adapt over time, providing personalized experiences that feel uniquely 'you'.

All this is just scratching the surface though; there's so much more potential waiting for us as we further explore what it means to fully embrace our digital aides in everyday life!

Unlocking the Full Potential of Your Digital Helper

Let's dive deeper into understanding how we can unlock the true potential of our digital helpers and make them an integral part of our lives.

It starts with embracing a simple truth: these AI-powered assistants are designed to do more than just tell you the weather or play your favorite songs. They're capable of becoming powerful tools that help us manage time, organize tasks, and even communicate more effectively.

Consider this - instead of juggling multiple apps for different tasks, wouldn't it be great if one assistant could handle everything?

Imagine waking up in the morning and simply saying 'Good morning' to your virtual assistant. In response, she not only wishes you back but also briefs you about your day— your schedule, reminders for important tasks—and even throws in a quick news update if you'd like!

She can book appointments for you, order groceries when they're running low, or remind you to call mom on her birthday. The key here is personalization; delve into your assistant's settings and preferences to tailor-make its capabilities according to what helps YOU the most.

So go ahead – take that leap! Explore beyond basic commands and get creative with how you interact with your digital helper. Train her to understand your habits better; set routines that trigger multiple actions with a single command; utilize her ability to integrate seamlessly across devices allowing smooth communication flow from home to office; teach her new skills available through updates or third-party apps.

You'll find yourself part of an exhilarating journey towards streamlined living where efficiency meets convenience at every turn.

Frequently Asked Questions

What are the privacy concerns associated with using virtual assistants like Siri or Alexa?

"Like a wolf in sheep's clothing, virtual assistants can be misleading. They may overhear private conversations, record personal data unknowingly and share it with third parties. You're not alone; we all tread this digital minefield."

How can these virtual assistants be integrated with other smart home devices?

You can seamlessly connect your virtual assistant to other smart home devices. Imagine, "Alexa, dim the lights."or "Hey Siri, turn up the heat."It's all about making your space feel more like you.

Are there any significant differences in the capabilities of different virtual assistants?

Yes, there are differences. While Siri excels at understanding natural language, Google Assistant is renowned for its accurate web searches. Alexa's strengths lie in smart home device integration. Each offers a unique experience.

How can I troubleshoot if my virtual assistant is not responding or working properly?

Don't worry! First, check your device's internet connection. Then, ensure the assistant's settings are correctly configured and updates are current. Restarting your device can also do wonders. You're not alone in this!

What is the impact of using virtual assistants on our cognitive or problem-solving skills?

"Using virtual assistants might give your brain a bit of a holiday. They can simplify tasks, but this may lead to less mental exercise and potentially dull your problem-solving skills over time. Stay engaged!"

Conclusion

So, you've grasped the reins of your modern-day genie, making life simpler by summoning Siri or Alexa's help. But don't rest on your laurels just yet! Keep exploring and you'll find these digital helpers can do more than add a dash of 21st-century magic to mundane chores.

Remember, we're not living in the Stone Age anymore. Unleash the full potential of AI and command your virtual assistant to bring convenience at your fingertips.

Embrace this brave new world with open arms!

Setting Up and Customizing Virtual Assistants to Meet Personal Needs

Ever felt like you're juggling too many things at once, wishing for an invisible helper to take some load off your shoulders?

Well, it's time to turn that wish into reality. In today's digital age, you don't need a magic lamp; all you need is a virtual assistant! These AI-powered helpers can organize your day, answer queries, play music on command and so much more - all tailored to your personal needs.

The best part? You're in control of how much (or little) they assist you with. With just a few settings and tweaks here and there, these virtual sidekicks can become an integral part of your routine.

This section will guide you through the process of setting up and customizing your own virtual assistant - from choosing the right one that fits your lifestyle to troubleshooting any issues that may arise along the way.

So let's dive in together into this world of convenience powered by artificial intelligence!

Key Takeaways
- Learning curve of setting up and customizing virtual assistants
- Personalizing virtual assistants to meet personal needs
- Overcoming challenges together strengthens bond
- Tap into discussed solutions

Choosing the Right AI Helper

When it comes to picking the right AI helper, you've got a lot to consider. You want a virtual assistant that fits seamlessly into your life, like a loyal companion who understands and anticipates your needs. Maybe you're the busy type who needs help managing your jam-packed calendar? Or perhaps you require an assistant with robust knowledge about cooking tips for those weekend culinary experiments?

The market is full of options from Google's Assistant to Amazon's Alexa, Apple's Siri, or Microsoft's Cortana; each with its unique strengths and capabilities. Remember that choosing an AI assistant isn't merely about what's popular or trendy. It's about finding the one that resonates most with your lifestyle and habits. Think of how exciting it would be to have an AI helper as part of your tribe - someone who can interact with you in a way that feels personalized and intimate.

Are you more conversational? Then maybe Siri with her chatty personality is right up your alley. If privacy is paramount for you, then perhaps Google Assistant might not be your first pick due to its data collection practices. Consider these aspects as if inviting a new member into your family because, in many ways, they will become part of your everyday life.

Now that we've explored some factors involved in choosing the perfect digital buddy, it's time to delve deeper into making this companion truly yours by focusing on setting up and personalizing their functions according to what makes sense for you. Remember though: this isn't just tech talk – it's about creating connections and feeling understood in our ever-evolving digital world. So let's move forward together towards understanding how initial configuration can make all the difference in fitting this digital aid smoothly into your daily routine.

Initial Configuration of Your Digital Aid

Navigating through the initial configuration of your digital aid can seem like threading a needle in the dark, but don't fret - it's not as challenging as you might think. You're about to join an ever-growing community of individuals who've successfully set up their own virtual assistants, bringing with them a sense of convenience and efficiency into their lives that they never thought possible.

Just imagine being part of this exciting new wave of technology users, experiencing firsthand how AI can streamline your tasks and help manage your everyday life.

Consider this your initiation ceremony into this modern tribe. The first step usually involves downloading the assistant app on your smart device or accessing it on your computer if it comes pre-installed. Next, you'll need to sign in or create a new account with basic information such as an email address and password.

Once you're signed in, the assistant will prompt you through a series of questions to understand your preferences better - helping it tailor its services more accurately to your needs. Remember every question is for building up its comprehension about you; there are no wrong answers here!

You're almost at the stage where you'll see just why everyone's raving about these digital aids! After going through these initial settings and getting familiar with its interface, remember that this tool is all about making life easier for you. So take some time exploring different features available within the app while anticipating our next discussion: personalizing these functions to fit seamlessly into your routine, transforming everyday tasks from mundane chores to effortless actions powered by advanced artificial intelligence.

Personalizing Assistant's Features

You'll be amazed at how these digital aids can be tailored to your unique lifestyle, making each day more productive and fulfilling. Your virtual assistant is just waiting to become an extension of you, reflecting your preferences, tastes, and habits.

Want it to play your favorite morning playlist as soon as you wake up? No problem! Need it to remind you about that big meeting coming up next week? Consider it done. With a few taps or spoken commands, they can adapt to your rhythm and routines.

Personalizing the features of your virtual assistant isn't only fun but also quite straightforward. Suppose you're a foodie who loves trying out new recipes; set up your assistant to fetch daily culinary inspiration from top chefs around the world. Maybe you're into fitness? Then instruct it to track your workouts and motivate you when those lazy days creep in!

You see, by adjusting its settings according to what matters most in your life, this technology becomes more than just a tool—it's like having a personal confidant that truly understands what makes you tick.

So now that we've covered how amazing personalizing these assistants can be for syncing with our daily lives, let's take things even further. The customization doesn't have to end here; believe it or not, there are ways for us all to tweak our digital companions' performance even more for optimal results!

Let's dive deeper into this fascinating journey of discovering how we can unlock the full potential of our virtual assistants.

Advanced Tweaking for Optimal Performance

Believe it or not, there's an entire world of advanced tweaking just waiting for you to explore, allowing your digital buddy to perform at its absolute best. You're not alone in this journey; countless tech enthusiasts and everyday users like yourself are diving into this realm, making their virtual assistants work smarter and harder for them.

The best part is that these tweaks aren't reserved only for the tech-savvy; they're accessible to anyone willing to take the time to understand their virtual assistant better.

In your pursuit of optimal performance, remember that customization is key. Your assistant should be a reflection of you - your needs, habits, and preferences. For example, did you know that most virtual assistants allow you to customize the wake-up phrase? Yes! Instead of the standard 'Hey Siri' or 'Okay Google', you can choose something unique that resonates more with your personality.

Moreover, many platforms offer access to developer options where you can fine-tune settings like speech recognition sensitivity or even enable power-saving modes when battery life is critical.

As much as we love our customized and highly efficient digital buddies, sometimes things might not go as smooth as we expect them. And when they don't - don't worry! Remember that every problem has a solution waiting on the other side.

This will lead us nicely into our next section, which focuses on troubleshooting common issues faced by users while using virtual assistants.

Troubleshooting Common Issues

Facing a hiccup with your digital buddy? Don't sweat it, we're about to dive into the most common issues and their solutions. Problems can range from simple things like not understanding commands to more complex issues like difficulty syncing with other devices. But remember, every problem has its solution; you just need to know where to look and how to fix it.

Here are some of the most common snags people hit when setting up and customizing their virtual assistants:

- **Misunderstanding or not recognizing commands:**

Make sure you're speaking clearly and using specific language.

Try adjusting the sensitivity settings if your assistant isn't picking up on your voice well.

Always check for updates as improvements in voice recognition happen regularly.

- **Difficulty connecting or syncing with other devices:**

Ensure both devices are compatible with each other.

Check that both devices have strong Wi-Fi connections.

Sometimes, a simple device restart can do wonders!

- **Privacy concerns:**

Regularly review and adjust your virtual assistant's privacy settings according to your comfort level.

Use command deletion features if sensitive information is accidentally recorded.

Remember, no tech journey is ever completely smooth sailing! These little hiccups are part of the learning curve that makes us tech-savvy explorers in our own right. So next time you hit an issue while setting up or customizing your virtual assistant, don't let frustration creep in. Instead, tap into these solutions we've discussed here today—you'll be back on track before you know it! After all, as part of this tech-loving community, overcoming challenges together only strengthens our bond!

Frequently Asked Questions

What are the privacy concerns when using virtual assistants?

You're right to consider privacy! Virtual assistants can potentially eavesdrop, record your conversations, and access personal data. They might even share this info with third parties. It's a real concern for our digital tribe!

How much does a typical virtual assistant cost?

You're probably wondering about the cost of a virtual assistant, right? Well, prices vary widely. Some are free like Google Assistant or Siri, while others may charge from $5 to hundreds per hour for specialized tasks.

Can virtual assistants be used on multiple devices simultaneously?

Absolutely! In fact, 51% of users utilize virtual assistants across multiple devices. You're part of a growing trend where folks enjoy seamless assistance no matter the device they're using at any given moment.

What languages do virtual assistants support?

You're in luck! Virtual assistants are multilingual and can support multiple languages including English, Spanish, French, German, Italian, Chinese and many more. It's like having a global companion right at your fingertips!

Are there any age restrictions for using virtual assistants?

Nope, there's no age limit to start using virtual assistants. They're designed for everyone! However, kids might need adult supervision while setting up. So, it doesn't matter how old you are - dive right in!

Conclusion

So, you've got your AI helper all set up and customized. It's no coincidence that your digital life feels more organized and efficient now, is it? That's the power of a well-tuned virtual assistant at work.

Remember, any issues you face are likely common ones with simple fixes. Don't let them discourage you. Keep tweaking until your digital aid is just right for you - after all, it's meant to make your life easier!

Leveraging Voice Commands for Everyday Activities, Such As Reminders, Weather Updates, and Navigation

In the hustle and bustle of your daily life, wouldn't it be nice to have a personal assistant at your beck and call? Imagine this: an assistant that never sleeps, never complains, is always ready for action, and best of all - fits right into your pocket.

Welcome to the world of virtual assistants! They're designed to make your life easier by handling tasks like setting alarms or reminders, providing weather updates, helping with navigation and so much more. All these services are provided hands-free as you only need to use voice commands.

Imagine how efficient you'd become if you could set a timer through speech while cooking or receive real-time climate information while planning your day out. What if you could get directions without taking your eyes off the road? Sounds magical, doesn't it?

Trust us; it's not magic but the power of technology at its finest. Virtual assistants leverage voice command technology to transform everyday activities into seamless tasks leaving you with more time for things that matter most in life.

So come along on this journey as we delve into how leveraging voice commands can revolutionize mundane chores into enjoyable experiences.

Key Takeaways

- Virtual assistants like Siri, Alexa, Cortana, and Google Assistant can perform everyday activities such as setting reminders, providing weather updates, and assisting with navigation through voice commands.
- Voice command technology is continuously evolving and becoming more accurate and intuitive, making interactions with virtual assistants feel more human-like.
- Virtual assistants can provide real-time climate information and directions, making planning and navigation easier for users.
- As artificial intelligence improves, voice recognition systems will become more seamless and integrated into routines, revolutionizing how we interact with our homes and control devices through voice commands.

The Emergence of Virtual Assistants

You've likely noticed the rise of virtual assistants in recent years, haven't you? They're transforming our daily routines and making mundane tasks like checking the weather or setting reminders a breeze.

From Siri to Alexa, Cortana to Google Assistant, these AI-powered pals are becoming part of our households, workplaces, and even on-the-go lifestyles. No need for typing or screen tapping; with just your voice command, they'll do the grunt work for you.

Think about it - how many times have you found yourself in need of an immediate weather update before heading out? Or maybe forgotten an important meeting because it slipped off your mind amidst a hectic day? Enter the world of virtual assistants! With their ability to understand and respond to voice commands accurately, they help keep your life organized while offering that touch of personalization.

Imagine asking Siri about today's weather and getting precise updates. And what about those reminders that pop up exactly when you want them? It feels like having a personal assistant who knows exactly what you need!

The convenience these virtual assistants bring is undeniably impressive. But remember, this is just scratching the surface as we explore their capabilities further. They can make calls for us; send emails; play our favorite music; provide news updates; help with cooking recipes...the list goes on! The best part? You don't have to be tech-savvy to leverage this technology - simply speak naturally!

As we delve deeper into understanding their potential uses in everyday activities such as setting alarms or timers via speech—the topic we'll touch upon next—there's no doubt that these AI companions will continue making our lives easier by leaps and bounds.

Setting Alarms and Timers via Speech

Imagine being able to set alarms and timers just by blurting out a sentence in the middle of your living room, it's almost like having magical powers! Now that virtual assistants have become a common part of our daily lives, this magic is very much real. Voice command technology takes convenience to another level.

You can be preparing dinner with messy hands and still manage to set a timer for the oven. Or maybe you're all cozy in bed and suddenly remember an important task for the next morning; no need to move, just say "Set an alarm for 7 am"and consider it done.

Voice-controlled assistants are not only making life easier but also fostering a sense of belonging as they respond instantly every time you call their name. There's something inherently comforting about having someone - or rather, something - always ready to assist you at any moment. It's like having your own personal helper who never tires or complains. And because these devices understand natural language, they make interactions feel more human-like than ever before.

So now that you've mastered the art of setting alarms and timers with your voice assistant, what's next? Well, there's more magic up its sleeve! Your voice assistant can also keep you updated with real-time climate information so that you're always prepared for whatever Mother Nature has in store. Whether it's going out dressed appropriately or planning indoor activities on rainy days – your voice assistant has got your back!

Receiving Real-Time Climate Information

Isn't it fantastic how your virtual assistant can keep you ahead of the game with real-time climate information? Whether you're planning a day trip or just dressing for the day, your voice-activated helper is there to provide up-to-the-minute weather updates. Just wake up and ask, 'Hey Assistant, what's the weather like today?' and voila! You'll get an instant response - no need to scroll through apps or wait for the morning news.

Imagine getting dressed without worrying about whether you've chosen the right outfit for the day's weather. With your virtual assistant at hand, that becomes a reality. You can walk out in confidence knowing that your clothing matches not only your style but also the forecasted conditions outside. It creates this comforting sense of belonging, knowing you're part of this grand tapestry of people who've used technology to make their lives simpler and more efficient.

But wait, there's more! Your digital companion isn't just here to tell you if it'll rain or shine – they can also guide you on your journey wherever you go. This power goes beyond merely informing; it keeps us connected to our environment and ensures we feel prepared every step of our journey.

As we move forward in leveraging these voice commands for everyday activities, let's explore how we could use them for hands-free directions and mapping as well.

Hands-Free Directions and Mapping

With your trusty virtual assistant by your side, getting lost is a thing of the past! Imagine driving to an unfamiliar location with the assurance that you'll reach your destination without any hiccups. Voice-activated technology makes this possible. Just say, 'Hey Assistant, take me to the nearest gas station,' or 'Navigate to 1234 Pine Street.' Your assistant will quickly pull up a map and start giving you turn-by-turn instructions.

You're no longer alone on your journey; it's like having a companion in the car who knows exactly where to go.

Life becomes even more convenient when using voice commands for public transit or walking directions. No need to fumble around with a paper map or try to decipher cryptic bus schedules anymore! Simply ask your digital buddy for help: 'What's the quickest route by bus?' or 'Guide me to the coffee shop on foot.' It's all about engaging with technology as if it were another person — not just a tool, but part of our everyday life gang!

Voice commands have revolutionized our navigation experiences, making them stress-free and enjoyable. But remember that this is only scratching the surface of what speech-based technology can do for us. As we look forward into uncharted territories, we can't help but get excited about what lies ahead in this ever-evolving tech landscape.

So buckle up and get ready for an exciting ride into the future of speech-based technology!

The Future of Speech-Based Technology

You've just begun to uncover the potential of speech-based technology, and it's clear that we are only at the dawn of this innovative era. The leaps and bounds that voice-command technology has made in recent years is staggering. They're not just about setting reminders or asking for weather updates anymore; they're moving towards becoming an integral part of our day-to-day lives, making them simpler and more efficient.

- Voice commands are expected to revolutionize how we interact with our homes - imagine walking into your house after a long day at work and simply saying 'lights on,' or telling your oven to preheat itself while you unwind.

- As artificial intelligence continues to evolve, so will the accuracy and intuitiveness of voice recognition systems. This means less frustration with misunderstood commands and more seamless integration into your routines.

- Furthermore, as security measures improve, you can expect voice-command capabilities to extend into more sensitive areas like banking or confidential business matters - think authorizing transactions with just your voice or dictating confidential emails without lifting a finger.

So picture this: a world where mundane tasks are dealt with a simple spoken command, leaving you free to engage in activities that truly matter. A world where technology feels less like an intruder and more like a helpful companion attuned to your needs. That's the future we're looking at with speech-based technology. It promises an inclusivity that goes beyond age or technological know-how because all it requires is for us to do what comes naturally – speak.

So get ready to embrace this innovation as it transforms everyday living into something extraordinary!

Frequently Asked Questions

How can voice commands be used to control smart home devices?

"You can command your smart home devices just by speaking! Imagine turning off lights, adjusting the thermostat, or playing music without lifting a finger. Feel connected to your space in a whole new way."

Can voice commands be used to make phone calls or send text messages?

Absolutely! Imagine shouting your thoughts into the wind, but instead of being lost, they're captured and turned into calls or texts. With voice commands, you're part of a world where communication becomes effortless.

Is there a way to customize the voice of my virtual assistant?

Absolutely! You're part of a group that values personalization. Most virtual assistants allow you to alter their voice, making your interactions uniquely yours. Check in the settings for options to customize your assistant's voice.

Are there any privacy concerns when using voice commands?

Absolutely, pal! When you're using voice commands, your words may be recorded or stored. This could pose privacy issues if these recordings are misused. So always ensure you trust the tech you're talking to.

Absolutely! Imagine settling on your couch, saying "Netflix, play Stranger Things,"and the next moment you're in Hawkins. Voice commands have made controlling TVs and entertainment systems more convenient than ever before.

Conclusion

You're probably imagining a world where you're the Tony Stark of your own story, casually asking Jarvis for weather updates or to set reminders. Well, that future isn't as far off as it seems.

With voice commands becoming increasingly sophisticated and integrated into our everyday lives, we're rapidly moving towards a hands-free, hassle-free era.

Embrace this wave of technological advancement and let your voice be the magic wand that simplifies your daily tasks!

Chapter 3: AI for Personal Productivity

Exploring AI-Powered Productivity Tools for Time Management and Organization

Like an hourglass with infinite sand, wouldn't you wish for a tool that can manage your time more efficiently?

As the world embraces the digital revolution, you're no longer confined to traditional methods of planning and organization. Welcome to the age of Artificial Intelligence (AI), where smart calendars and AI-assisted apps have become your allies in navigating through chaotic schedules and tasks.

This isn't just about staying on top of your game; it's about being part of a community that recognizes the power of technology in enhancing productivity.

Dive into this exploration of AI-powered productivity tools - from streamlining everyday tasks to providing personalized suggestions for improved workflow. You'll discover how these innovations are transforming not only our individual work habits but also reshaping the future landscape of work itself.

With automation and AI at its core, envision a workspace where efficiency meets convenience. Remember, you're not alone in this journey towards better time management and organization; we're all embracing this new era together.

Key Takeaways
- AI-powered tools revolutionize daily tasks and save time and energy.
- AI-powered tools offer personalized suggestions and help prioritize tasks.
- AI-powered tools contribute to increased efficiency and productivity.
- The future of work involves automation and AI acting as personal advisors for peak potential.

Understanding AI and Its Role in Efficiency

You'll be amazed at how AI can revolutionize your daily tasks, turning monotonous chores into efficient processes that save you time and energy. Just imagine, instead of sifting through hundreds of emails to find the one document you need, an AI-powered tool could do it for you in seconds. That's the power of artificial intelligence; it learns from your behavior and patterns over time, making its performance even more effective as it goes along. It's like having a personal assistant who knows exactly what you need before even asking.

Being part of a community that embraces such innovation is exciting! Think about all those minutes wasted on repetitive tasks now being put to better use. The beauty of these tools isn't just their efficiency but also their ability to free up mental space so you can focus on more important matters - be it work-related or personal pursuits. With AI working like a charm in the background, you don't have to sweat the small stuff anymore.

You're not alone in this either: countless individuals and businesses are reaping the benefits of integrating AI tools into their routines, forging a sense of belonging among users.

The future is here with AI powering our productivity tools for maximum efficiency and organization. Beyond just sorting out your inbox, these smart solutions are transforming calendars too—making scheduling seamless while ensuring nothing slips through the cracks. So if keeping track of appointments has been a challenge for you or your team—fret not!

This marks an entranceway into our next discussion about 'the rise of smart calendars', where we delve deeper into how technology continues to shape our lives for the better.

The Rise of Smart Calendars

Did you know that, according to a study by RescueTime, people who use smart calendars save an average of 15% more time compared to those who don't? Smart calendars are becoming increasingly popular as the demand for better time management and organization tools grows. These AI-powered tools can do much more than just remind you of your meetings; they analyze your schedule, suggest optimal times for tasks based on your patterns, and even automatically set reminders. It's like having a personal assistant right in your pocket!

Surely, being part of a community that utilizes such innovative technology makes one feel modern and efficient. You're not alone in this; many individuals and businesses have embraced these smart calendars because they offer what traditional ones cannot - flexibility and optimization. They adapt to your unique schedule, ensuring no two days look exactly alike unless you want them to be. You can easily reschedule appointments or add new ones without disrupting the rest of your day.

Plus, with features like traffic predictions and meeting buffers built-in, it's easier than ever to plan ahead.

Imagine how much smoother life would be if all our tasks were neatly organized into manageable slots in our day! That's precisely the promise offered by smart calendars – less chaos, more control. And remember: using these tools isn't about being rigid or overly structured; it's about creating an environment where productivity thrives naturally. So why not take advantage of these advancements? The benefits extend beyond just saving time; they also create space for creativity and innovation to flourish unimpeded by daily minutiae.

As we delve deeper into AI-assisted applications next, think about how transformative integrating such technologies could be for managing tasks at home or work.

Streamlining Tasks with AI-Assisted Apps

It's remarkable how AI-assisted apps can transform the way we handle daily tasks, offering seamless solutions that automate and simplify even the most complex activities. These smart tools are designed to streamline your workflow, making sure you're able to maximize productivity without feeling overwhelmed. Whether it's sorting your emails or scheduling meetings, these apps have got you covered.

- **Task Automation:** AI-powered applications such as RescueTime and Todoist help you manage your tasks efficiently. They can automatically categorize your tasks based on priority and deadline, allowing you to focus more on completion rather than organization.

- **Email Sorting:** Tools like Spark and Sanebox use artificial intelligence to declutter your inbox by sorting out important emails from promotional ones.

- **Meeting Scheduling:** Clara, an intelligent personal assistant app, schedules meetings for you based on the availability of all participants.

- **Project Management:** Software like Trello uses AI algorithms to provide insights into project timelines, helping teams stay aligned with their goals.

By taking advantage of these brilliant tools that technology offers us today, we don't just become more efficient - we also find ourselves belonging to a community that values innovation and progress. We become part of a world where work-life balance isn't just achievable but is the norm. As we embrace these powerful resources at our fingertips, we notice a significant change in our time management skills and overall productivity level.

Moving forward with enhanced time management techniques through AI-powered tools doesn't end here! There's another aspect that further boosts efficiency – personalized suggestions based on individual habits and preferences. In fact, imagine using an app that knows when you're most productive during the day or what kind of tasks take up too much of your time? Stay tuned as we delve into this exciting new frontier next.

Personalized Suggestions for Enhanced Workflow

Imagine an app that, like a trusted friend, understands your work habits and preferences and provides personalized recommendations to enhance your workflow. Think about those moments when you're feeling stuck or overwhelmed by the myriad of tasks ahead of you. Only for this intuitive tool to swoop in and offer targeted suggestions on how best to allocate your time and energy.

This isn't just any ordinary productivity app; it's one powered by artificial intelligence that learns from your patterns and adjusts its advice accordingly. It's like having a personal assistant who knows exactly what you need before you even realize it yourself.

Now picture the freedom this could grant you! With this smart companion by your side, no task would seem too daunting anymore. You'd be able to prioritize efficiently, manage deadlines with ease, and navigate through the most hectic days with serene confidence.

The AI not only helps keep track of what needs doing but also intelligently suggests ways to make the process smoother. Perhaps recommending quiet hours in the day when you can focus on difficult tasks or identifying recurring activities that could be batched together for efficiency.

But let's not stop at imagining; such AI-powered tools are already transforming our present workspaces into more efficient environments. As we move forward into an era where automation and artificial intelligence play pivotal roles in shaping industries worldwide, they promise new possibilities for optimizing productivity like never before.

The future of work is one where these intelligent systems aid us in harnessing our potential better than ever before – ushering us towards unprecedented efficiency and balance between our professional and personal lives.

And so, as we stand on the brink of this exciting evolution in workplace dynamics...

The Future of Work with Automation and AI

We're on the cusp of a revolutionary shift in work dynamics, where automation and artificial intelligence don't just take up mundane tasks, but also act as our personal advisors, guiding us to reach our peak potential.

Imagine a future where you're not drowning in paperwork or stuck in endless meetings. Instead, your AI assistant has already sorted out your schedule, prioritized your tasks according to their urgency and importance, and is now offering you expert insights to solve that project dilemma you've been wrestling with.

This is not some distant utopia; it's an emerging reality being shaped by AI-powered productivity tools. These tools are designed to learn from your behavior patterns over time and provide personalized strategies for efficient time management and organization.

Think about how transformative this could be! Gone will be the days of feeling overwhelmed by your workload or scrambling at the last minute due to poor planning. You'll feel more connected with your work rhythm than ever before, knowing there's a smart system backing you up every step of the way.

But here's the real kicker: along with boosting productivity and efficiency at individual levels, these advancements promise major impacts on organizational culture too. Businesses can look forward to more engaged employees who are better equipped to handle complex challenges — all thanks to artificial intelligence smoothing out kinks in time management and workflow optimization.

It's like having a motivational team member who always knows how best to support you while simultaneously driving company-wide growth agendas forward! So stand tall as part of this exciting evolution; after all, we're all shaping this brave new world together!

Frequently Asked Questions

How can AI-powered productivity tools affect the work-life balance?

Did you know 40% of people report improved work-life balance using AI tools? They help you manage tasks efficiently, leaving more time for your personal life. You'll feel part of a productive, balanced world!

Can AI-powered tools replace human involvement in time management and organization?

Absolutely! AI-powered tools can streamline your time management and organization tasks. However, they can't completely replace human intuition and judgment. Embrace the tech, but remember you're still the boss of your own time!

What are some potential privacy concerns related to using AI-powered productivity tools?

You may worry about AI tools accessing your personal info, like emails or schedules. There's also the risk of data breaches and misuse by third parties. It's crucial to use trusted tools with solid privacy policies.

How do AI-powered tools integrate with existing non-AI systems in the workplace?

Like a skilled conductor, AI-powered tools harmonize with your existing systems. They're designed to weave seamlessly into the fabric of your workspace, enhancing efficiency without disrupting the rhythm of your current operations.

Are there any specific industries that benefit more from using AI-powered productivity tools?

Absolutely! Industries with large volumes of data like healthcare, finance, and tech greatly benefit from AI tools. They help you save time, streamline processes and facilitate better decision-making. It's a game-changer for many!

Conclusion

So, you're standing at the dawn of a new era. AI-powered tools aren't just reshaping the way we work—they're revolutionizing it. They're like your personal backstage crew, orchestrating your tasks while you take the spotlight.

Don't be fooled, this isn't a fleeting trend. Welcome to your future workplace—efficient, personalized, and streamlined to perfection. Embrace AI as it ushers in a brave new world of productivity and time management!

Using AI-Based Task Managers and Scheduling Apps for Improved Efficiency

Imagine you're a seasoned conductor, orchestrating the symphony of your everyday life. Each task is an instrument, each deadline a note, and together they create the music that drives your productivity. Now imagine if you had a tool to fine-tune this orchestra - one that not only keeps time with precision but also learns and adapts to your rhythm.

That's where AI-based task managers and scheduling apps come in. According to research from Accenture, artificial intelligence could boost productivity by 40% in less than two decades. The promise of such advancement begs exploration into how AI can help streamline our daily activities, send personalized notifications and reminders, adapt to our work habits, and ultimately improve efficiency.

It's like having a virtual assistant who understands you better as you spend more time together - making sure you feel supported while helping you hit all the right notes in your personal productivity composition.

So let's delve into understanding these modern maestros better!

Key Takeaways

- AI-based task managers and scheduling apps can boost productivity by 40% in less than two decades, according to research from Accenture.
- These tools streamline daily activities, taking over mundane tasks and allowing users to focus on what matters most.
- AI-based task managers and scheduling apps learn from user routines and habits, offering personalized suggestions to work smarter.
- These tools prioritize tasks based on urgency and importance, aligning them with users' peak performance times.

Understanding the Mechanics of AI Tools

Let's dive right into understanding how these AI tools actually work, shall we? It's not as complicated as you might think!

Essentially, AI-based task managers and scheduling apps operate on a set of algorithms that have been designed to learn from your behavior. They analyze the data inputted, recognize patterns, and then make predictions or decisions based on their learning. This could be anything from suggesting an optimal time for a meeting considering everyone's schedules to reminding you about tasks based on when you've completed similar ones in the past.

You're never alone with these AI tools by your side – they're like your personal digital assistants who know what you need before even you do! For instance, if you have a big presentation due at the end of the week, your AI app will remind you to start working on it early in order to meet the deadline. It might even suggest breaking down large tasks into smaller ones, making them seem less overwhelming. The beauty lies in how these apps adapt and evolve according to your habits and preferences over time – all thanks to machine learning, which is at the heart of their operation!

And just imagine this: As weeks pass by using these intelligent services, there's an unseen bond developing between you and this technology. You'll find that it becomes easier than ever before to manage daily routines efficiently without any stress or strain.

So now that we understand how these AI-based task managers function, let's see how they can help streamline our day-to-day activities in ways we'd never imagined possible!

Streamlining Daily Activities

Streamlining daily activities with modern tools is like having a personal assistant who's more efficient than a thousand secretaries combined. Imagine the relief you'll feel when your workload lightens, and there's finally time to breathe, to think, to create.

These AI-based task managers aren't just gadgets; they're companions in your quest for productivity. They take over mundane tasks that would otherwise consume precious hours of your day, enabling you to focus on what truly matters.

In this digital age where everyone is part of the global village, it's easy to feel overwhelmed by the sheer volume of tasks and responsibilities thrown at us daily. This is where AI scheduling apps step in - not as mere tools but as allies that understand your unique routines and habits. They learn from you every day, adjusting their algorithms accordingly so they can offer personalized suggestions designed to help you work smarter, not harder. You're not alone in this journey; you've got a reliable partner backing you up.

As these intelligent tools continue to evolve and adapt with each passing day, they become increasingly adept at handling complex schedules and diverse sets of tasks. Beyond simple reminders or calendar entries, they provide analytical insights into how best utilize your time based on past patterns and preferences.

And guess what? This seamless integration doesn't stop here – it extends beyond managing tasks and into keeping track of important dates or meetings through personalized notifications and reminders which we will explore next.

Personalized Notifications and Reminders

In today's fast-paced world, personalized notifications and reminders are like your very own digital personal assistant, always on hand to keep you on track. Imagine never having to worry about forgetting important tasks or appointments because your AI-based task manager is there to do the remembering for you. It's akin to having a trusted friend who knows your schedule inside out and nudges you at the right time.

You're not alone in this; we all yearn for a system that makes life easier and keeps us connected with our responsibilities.

AI-based task managers go beyond just setting alarms; they learn from your habits, making them more aware of when it's best to remind you of upcoming tasks. For instance, if you're a night owl getting most of your work done after sunset, it won't bother you with reminders during the day when it knows you're less productive. It understands that everybody marches to their own beat and tailors its approach accordingly. You'll feel understood and supported as it helps navigate through your daily routine seamlessly.

Personalized notifications and reminders can indeed make a significant difference in managing your time effectively while providing a sense of belonging - knowing there's an intelligent tool tailored specifically for your needs.

Now let's delve deeper into how these tools adapt further by adjusting not only according to what works best for you but also by continually learning from your work patterns and habits over time.

Adapting to Your Work Habits

Ever feel like you're channeling Bill Murray in Groundhog Day, stuck in a loop of repeated tasks and routines? That's where personalized notifications and reminders come into play, adapting to your work habits like a chameleon changing its colors. AI-based task managers and scheduling apps are designed to do just that - learn from your patterns and customize themselves accordingly.

They become an extension of you, mirroring your workflow and understanding when you're most productive or what times of the day you prefer certain activities. It's as if they transform into a personal assistant that knows how you operate better than anyone else.

Imagine having an app that can predict when you'll need a break based on your past behavior or suggest the best time for brainstorming sessions because it has observed that's when your creativity peaks. Sounds too good to be true? With AI technology embedded within these tools, they make it possible!

Not only this but think about how valuable it would be if these apps could also prioritize tasks based on their urgency and importance, aligning them with your peak performance times. The idea is not about taking away control but giving more power to you by enabling smarter decision-making.

The real beauty of using AI-based task managers is their ability to adapt continually. As we evolve in our roles, responsibilities or simply as individuals, so does the tool learning along with us. It's almost as if there's a constant conversation happening between you and the app: helping each other grow smarter every day!

This symbiosis doesn't merely improve efficiency; it revolutionizes the way we perceive productivity altogether. Now let's delve deeper by evaluating how this impacts productivity levels across different aspects of work-life balance.

Evaluating the Impact on Productivity

When we're assessing the effect on productivity, it's clear that these personalized tools don't just change how we work—they redefine what it means to be truly productive.

With AI-based task managers and scheduling apps, you're not merely keeping track of tasks; you're harnessing the power of artificial intelligence to shape your day-to-day activities. These applications intelligently sort through your commitments, prioritize them based on your preferences and deadlines, and offer suggestions for the best ways to accomplish them.

Suddenly, being productive isn't about doing more—it's about doing what matters most effectively.

Just imagine: no more fumbling around with sticky notes or wrestling with unwieldy spreadsheets. Instead, you've got a virtual assistant who knows you better than anyone else—understanding your work patterns, recognizing when you're most alert and creative, even anticipating tasks before they hit your plate.

As a result, stress decreases as efficiency increases—you begin to feel part of an empowered community where everyone has their personal AI tool designed to help manage their time better.

Experience shows us that users of AI-based task managers find themselves accomplishing more in less time while also boosting their quality of work. They report feeling less overwhelmed by their workload while simultaneously achieving a greater sense of accomplishment in their daily tasks.

It's like joining an exclusive club where members are thriving instead of surviving – working smarter rather than harder. You too can become part of this transformational shift towards enhanced productivity facilitated by technology!

Frequently Asked Questions

What is the cost of implementing AI-based task managers and scheduling apps in a business setting?

Costs of AI-based task managers can vary greatly. You'll be investing in efficiency, but that initial price tag could be steep. Remember, though, you're not just buying an app - you're joining a productivity revolution!

How secure are these AI-based task management tools and what measures are in place to protect user data?

Like a vault guarding precious jewels, AI-based task managers ensure top-notch security. They use encryption, two-factor authentication and regular audits to protect your data. You're not just using an app, you're joining a safe community.

Can AI-based task managers and scheduling apps be integrated with other digital tools that I currently use?

Absolutely! Your AI-based task manager can seamlessly integrate with your current digital tools, creating a harmonious tech ecosystem. You'll feel connected and efficient, part of a bigger community using smart solutions for productivity.

Are there any notable companies or organizations that have successfully implemented these AI tools for improved efficiency?

"Success leaves clues. Big names like IBM, Google, and Microsoft are trailblazers in implementing AI-based task managers and scheduling tools. You're not alone in embracing this efficiency revolution; you're part of a bigger picture."

What kind of technical support is available for users who encounter issues with these AI-based task managers and scheduling apps?

You're not alone in this tech adventure! Most AI task manager and scheduling apps offer robust customer service, including 24/7 live chat, email support, and even community forums for shared wisdom.

Conclusion

You've seen how AI-based task managers and scheduling apps can revolutionize your work life. They don't just automate tasks, they learn from you, adapt to your habits, and help streamline daily activities.

Imagine the boost in productivity when these smart tools are integrated into your routine. The theory is clear: AI has the power to transform mundane tasks into efficient processes.

So why not embrace it and let technology take the reins?

Using AI-Based Task Managers and Scheduling Apps for Improved Efficiency

Imagine you're a seasoned conductor, orchestrating the symphony of your everyday life. Each task is an instrument, each deadline a note, and together they create the music that drives your productivity. Now imagine if you had a tool to fine-tune this orchestra - one that not only keeps time with precision but also learns and adapts to your rhythm.

That's where AI-based task managers and scheduling apps come in. According to research from Accenture, artificial intelligence could boost productivity by 40% in less than two decades. The promise of such advancement begs exploration into how AI can help streamline our daily activities, send personalized notifications and reminders, adapt to our work habits, and ultimately improve efficiency.

It's like having a virtual assistant who understands you better as you spend more time together - making sure you feel supported while helping you hit all the right notes in your personal productivity composition.

So let's delve into understanding these modern maestros better!

Key Takeaways

- AI-based task managers and scheduling apps can boost productivity by 40% in less than two decades, according to research from Accenture.
- These tools streamline daily activities, taking over mundane tasks and allowing users to focus on what matters most.
- AI-based task managers and scheduling apps learn from user routines and habits, offering personalized suggestions to work smarter.
- These tools prioritize tasks based on urgency and importance, aligning them with users' peak performance times.

Understanding the Mechanics of AI Tools

Let's dive right into understanding how these AI tools actually work, shall we? It's not as complicated as you might think!

Essentially, AI-based task managers and scheduling apps operate on a set of algorithms that have been designed to learn from your behavior. They analyze the data inputted, recognize patterns, and then make predictions or decisions based on their learning. This could be anything from suggesting an optimal time for a meeting considering everyone's schedules to reminding you about tasks based on when you've completed similar ones in the past.

You're never alone with these AI tools by your side – they're like your personal digital assistants who know what you need before even you do! For instance, if you have a big presentation due at the end of the week, your AI app will remind you to start working on it early in order to meet the deadline. It might even suggest breaking down large tasks into smaller ones, making them seem less overwhelming. The beauty lies in how these apps adapt and evolve according to your habits and preferences over time – all thanks to machine learning, which is at the heart of their operation!

And just imagine this: As weeks pass by using these intelligent services, there's an unseen bond developing between you and this technology. You'll find that it becomes easier than ever before to manage daily routines efficiently without any stress or strain.

So now that we understand how these AI-based task managers function, let's see how they can help streamline our day-to-day activities in ways we'd never imagined possible!

Streamlining Daily Activities

Streamlining daily activities with modern tools is like having a personal assistant who's more efficient than a thousand secretaries combined. Imagine the relief you'll feel when your workload lightens, and there's finally time to breathe, to think, to create.

These AI-based task managers aren't just gadgets; they're companions in your quest for productivity. They take over mundane tasks that would otherwise consume precious hours of your day, enabling you to focus on what truly matters.

In this digital age where everyone is part of the global village, it's easy to feel overwhelmed by the sheer volume of tasks and responsibilities thrown at us daily. This is where AI scheduling apps step in - not as mere tools but as allies that understand your unique routines and habits. They learn from you every day, adjusting their algorithms accordingly so they can offer personalized suggestions designed to help you work smarter, not harder. You're not alone in this journey; you've got a reliable partner backing you up.

As these intelligent tools continue to evolve and adapt with each passing day, they become increasingly adept at handling complex schedules and diverse sets of tasks. Beyond simple reminders or calendar entries, they provide analytical insights into how best utilize your time based on past patterns and preferences.

And guess what? This seamless integration doesn't stop here – it extends beyond managing tasks and into keeping track of important dates or meetings through personalized notifications and reminders which we will explore next.

Personalized Notifications and Reminders

In today's fast-paced world, personalized notifications and reminders are like your very own digital personal assistant, always on hand to keep you on track. Imagine never having to worry about forgetting important tasks or appointments because your AI-based task manager is there to do the remembering for you. It's akin to having a trusted friend who knows your schedule inside out and nudges you at the right time.

You're not alone in this; we all yearn for a system that makes life easier and keeps us connected with our responsibilities.

AI-based task managers go beyond just setting alarms; they learn from your habits, making them more aware of when it's best to remind you of upcoming tasks. For instance, if you're a night owl getting most of your work done after sunset, it won't bother you with reminders during the day when it knows you're less productive. It understands that everybody marches to their own beat and tailors its approach accordingly. You'll feel understood and supported as it helps navigate through your daily routine seamlessly.

Personalized notifications and reminders can indeed make a significant difference in managing your time effectively while providing a sense of belonging - knowing there's an intelligent tool tailored specifically for your needs.

Now let's delve deeper into how these tools adapt further by adjusting not only according to what works best for you but also by continually learning from your work patterns and habits over time.

Adapting to Your Work Habits

Ever feel like you're channeling Bill Murray in Groundhog Day, stuck in a loop of repeated tasks and routines? That's where personalized notifications and reminders come into play, adapting to your work habits like a chameleon changing its colors. AI-based task managers and scheduling apps are designed to do just that - learn from your patterns and customize themselves accordingly.

They become an extension of you, mirroring your workflow and understanding when you're most productive or what times of the day you prefer certain activities. It's as if they transform into a personal assistant that knows how you operate better than anyone else.

Imagine having an app that can predict when you'll need a break based on your past behavior or suggest the best time for brainstorming sessions because it has observed that's when your creativity peaks. Sounds too good to be true? With AI technology embedded within these tools, they make it possible!

Not only this but think about how valuable it would be if these apps could also prioritize tasks based on their urgency and importance, aligning them with your peak performance times. The idea is not about taking away control but giving more power to you by enabling smarter decision-making.

The real beauty of using AI-based task managers is their ability to adapt continually. As we evolve in our roles, responsibilities or simply as individuals, so does the tool learning along with us. It's almost as if there's a constant conversation happening between you and the app: helping each other grow smarter every day!

This symbiosis doesn't merely improve efficiency; it revolutionizes the way we perceive productivity altogether. Now let's delve deeper by evaluating how this impacts productivity levels across different aspects of work-life balance.

Evaluating the Impact on Productivity

When we're assessing the effect on productivity, it's clear that these personalized tools don't just change how we work—they redefine what it means to be truly productive.

With AI-based task managers and scheduling apps, you're not merely keeping track of tasks; you're harnessing the power of artificial intelligence to shape your day-to-day activities. These applications intelligently sort through your commitments, prioritize them based on your preferences and deadlines, and offer suggestions for the best ways to accomplish them.

Suddenly, being productive isn't about doing more—it's about doing what matters most effectively.

Just imagine: no more fumbling around with sticky notes or wrestling with unwieldy spreadsheets. Instead, you've got a virtual assistant who knows you better than anyone else—understanding your work patterns, recognizing when you're most alert and creative, even anticipating tasks before they hit your plate.

As a result, stress decreases as efficiency increases—you begin to feel part of an empowered community where everyone has their personal AI tool designed to help manage their time better.

Experience shows us that users of AI-based task managers find themselves accomplishing more in less time while also boosting their quality of work. They report feeling less overwhelmed by their workload while simultaneously achieving a greater sense of accomplishment in their daily tasks.

It's like joining an exclusive club where members are thriving instead of surviving – working smarter rather than harder. You too can become part of this transformational shift towards enhanced productivity facilitated by technology!

Frequently Asked Questions

What is the cost of implementing AI-based task managers and scheduling apps in a business setting?

Costs of AI-based task managers can vary greatly. You'll be investing in efficiency, but that initial price tag could be steep. Remember, though, you're not just buying an app - you're joining a productivity revolution!

How secure are these AI-based task management tools and what measures are in place to protect user data?

Like a vault guarding precious jewels, AI-based task managers ensure top-notch security. They use encryption, two-factor authentication and regular audits to protect your data. You're not just using an app, you're joining a safe community.

Can AI-based task managers and scheduling apps be integrated with other digital tools that I currently use?

Absolutely! Your AI-based task manager can seamlessly integrate with your current digital tools, creating a harmonious tech ecosystem. You'll feel connected and efficient, part of a bigger community using smart solutions for productivity.

Are there any notable companies or organizations that have successfully implemented these AI tools for improved efficiency?

"Success leaves clues. Big names like IBM, Google, and Microsoft are trailblazers in implementing AI-based task managers and scheduling tools. You're not alone in embracing this efficiency revolution; you're part of a bigger picture."

What kind of technical support is available for users who encounter issues with these AI-based task managers and scheduling apps?

You're not alone in this tech adventure! Most AI task manager and scheduling apps offer robust customer service, including 24/7 live chat, email support, and even community forums for shared wisdom.

Conclusion

You've seen how AI-based task managers and scheduling apps can revolutionize your work life. They don't just automate tasks, they learn from you, adapt to your habits, and help streamline daily activities.

Imagine the boost in productivity when these smart tools are integrated into your routine. The theory is clear: AI has the power to transform mundane tasks into efficient processes.

So why not embrace it and let technology take the reins?

Integrating AI-Driven Note-Taking and Document Management Systems

You've probably heard the buzz about artificial intelligence (AI) revolutionizing business operations. But what if I told you that AI can do more than just automate tasks?

Imagine a world where your note-taking and document management systems are driven by AI, leaving you with more time to focus on the things that really matter in your work. From automatically transcribing meeting minutes to organizing documents efficiently, AI tools have the potential to transform the way you work.

But integrating AI into your daily routine is not as simple as it sounds. You'll need to understand its capabilities, align these tools with your work processes, train your team on how to use them effectively and make adjustments along the way.

Don't worry though - we're here every step of the way! We'll break down each stage in detail so that you feel right at home when adopting these new tech-savvy tools. So let's embark on this exciting journey together towards maximizing efficiency and productivity at our workplaces using AI-driven systems!

Key Takeaways

- AI-driven note-taking and document management systems automate tasks and increase productivity.
- These systems capture important details automatically and organize files efficiently using AI algorithms.
- AI technology revolutionizes daily work routines by handling tasks like meeting scheduling, email drafting, and document organization.
- Integrating AI systems should feel natural and seamless, becoming second nature for improved efficiency.

Understanding the Capabilities of AI Tools

You'll be amazed to see how AI tools can automatically transcribe your spoken words, organize your notes, and even sift through mountains of documents in a snap. The smartest tech firms globally have been working tirelessly to perfect algorithms that understand human language.

By integrating an AI-driven note-taking system into your workflow, you're no longer just keeping up with the times; you're ahead of the curve. These innovative tools will meticulously sort out your information, creating a digital oasis amidst the desert of data. You're not just adopting technology; you're embracing an ally that works for you.

Imagine being part of a community where everyone functions at their optimum level because they have top-notch AI tools at their disposal - Sounds enticing, isn't it? This is more than just about efficiency or productivity; it's about being part of something bigger. It's about belonging to a future-forward tribe that leverages technology to maximize potential and unleash creativity.

With AI document management systems in place, say goodbye to hoarding piles of paperwork and hello to streamlined operations.

As we venture further into this discussion, remember that while these tools are indeed revolutionary, they aren't magic wands—they need strategic alignment with work processes for maximum effectiveness.

So now let's delve deeper into how these AI tools can enhance our productivity by aligning them properly with our work processes without taking any missteps on this exciting journey towards optimization!

Aligning AI Tools with Work Processes

Incorporating advanced technology into work processes can be a game-changer, but it's essential to ensure these tools align seamlessly with your existing workflows.

Imagine having an AI-driven note-taking and document management system that understands your business lingo, acts as your personal assistant, and keeps everything organized without requiring you to change how you work. Isn't that exciting?

With the right alignment in place, these systems can take over mundane tasks like sorting emails or organizing notes from meetings. This leaves you with more time to focus on what truly matters – driving forward the goals of your organization.

Now picture yourself collaborating with colleagues in real-time using these AI tools - sharing ideas, brainstorming solutions to challenges, and drafting strategies for success. You won't feel lost anymore amidst piles of documents or unending threads of emails because your AI tool will always have your back! It will keep track of all discussions, retrieve information when needed, and even generate summaries after each meeting. It'll be like having another team member who never sleeps!

But remember, it's not just about getting the best AI tool out there; it's about making sure it fits well within your existing workflow so everyone feels comfortable using it. And once this happens, you're not only part of a well-oiled machine but also part of a community that embraces innovation for increased productivity and success.

So don't wait around! The next challenge is ensuring everyone learns how to make the most out of this amazing piece of technology efficiently – get ready to train your team on AI systems!

Training Your Team on AI Systems

It's crucial that we're up to speed with how to use these advanced tools effectively, as they can revolutionize not only our individual tasks but also how we collaborate as a team. AI-driven note-taking and document management systems are no exception. They're designed to make our lives easier, boosting productivity and enabling us to focus on what truly matters – the core of our work.

However, like any other tool, their effectiveness depends largely on how well we understand and utilize them.

- Firstly, it's important for everyone in the team to undergo training sessions where they learn about:
- The basic functions of the system: This includes understanding how the system records notes, organizes documents, or performs any other primary features.
- Advanced functionalities: Once everyone is comfortable with the basics, moving onto more complex features can unlock even greater potential from these AI tools.
- Troubleshooting common issues: No system is perfect; understanding how to resolve typical problems ensures minimal disruption in workflow when they occur.

Secondly, ongoing support should be provided after initial training. This might involve periodic refresher courses or having an expert available for queries.

Lastly, each team member should be encouraged to explore and experiment with the system independently. Remember that learning by doing is often one of the best ways to master new technology.

Knowing your way around AI systems isn't just about getting work done faster or more efficiently—it's also about feeling confident in your ability to navigate this brave new world of work technology. It's about being part of a modern workforce that harnesses innovation for collective success.

So take this knowledge you've gained from training into practice; immerse yourself fully into using these systems daily in your tasks and interactions with colleagues. As we transition smoothly into discussing implementing AI in your daily work routine next time around, remember it all starts with you making an effort today!

Implementing AI in Your Daily Work Routine

Ready to revolutionize your workday with the magic of artificial intelligence? That's right, we're diving headfirst into a world where your daily tasks are supercharged by cutting-edge technology.

Picture this: you're sipping your morning coffee as AI handles your meeting scheduling, email drafting, and document organization. It's more than mere convenience; it's an entirely new level of productivity that leaves more room for creative thinking and innovation.

Imagine having an AI-driven note-taking system that captures salient points from every meeting or conference call automatically. You don't have to worry about missing critical details or mishearing instructions anymore.

A similar approach can be taken with document management systems. These smart systems not only store files but also organize them efficiently using AI algorithms, making retrieval a breeze. And yes, they do understand context! So when you search for a keyword, the system brings up all relevant files - even those where the keyword isn't explicitly mentioned but is contextually relevant.

This new reality doesn't just make work easier; it makes us better at our jobs by freeing up mental space for strategic thought and creativity. The potential benefits are limitless as we continue to explore how to best use these tools in our everyday work routines.

Now that we've established how seamlessly you can incorporate AI into your daily routine, let's shift gears and discuss how one might maximize the potential of these transformative AI systems in greater detail.

Maximizing the Potential of AI Systems

Harnessing the full potential of these revolutionary tech tools requires a strategic approach and understanding of their capabilities. Remember, you're part of an exciting global community embracing this cutting-edge technology - so don't be left behind!

Start by familiarizing yourself with the features and functions of your AI-driven note-taking and document management systems. Learn how to use them effectively in different scenarios, whether it's for work or personal use. Aim to maximize the benefits they offer like auto-tagging relevant information, summarizing lengthy documents, or transcribing meetings accurately.

One of the most significant advantages you can leverage is automation. Imagine being part of a connected network where mundane tasks are simplified, leaving you more time to focus on strategic thinking and creativity - sounds fantastic, right?

With AI systems automating routine tasks such as organizing files or generating reports based on notes taken automatically, you can streamline workflows like never before. This not only increases productivity but also reduces errors caused by manual processes.

Remember that getting the most out of these advanced tools isn't just about understanding how they work; it's about making them work for you. Adopting an AI system into your daily routine should feel natural rather than forced. Integration should be seamless so that it becomes second nature to rely on these tools for improved efficiency in your day-to-day life.

Embrace this new norm confidently, knowing that you're ahead in reaping the benefits from this technological revolution. After all, being part of progress feels empowering, doesn't it?

Frequently Asked Questions

What are the costs associated with integrating AI-driven note-taking and document management systems?

"Did you know businesses spend around $20K per user on document management annually? You'll invest in AI-driven note-taking and document systems, but imagine the cost savings! Be part of a progressive, smarter working world."

How is data privacy ensured when using AI-driven systems for note-taking and document management?

You're part of a community that values data privacy, aren't you? AI-driven systems ensure this by using encryption, strict access controls and regular audits. Your notes and documents are safe, making you feel right at home.

Can AI-driven note-taking systems be used across different platforms and devices?

Absolutely! Your AI note-taking buddy isn't picky. It'll happily hop from your laptop to your smartphone, even to your tablet. Making notes will feel like a party where everyone's invited!

What are the potential risks and challenges associated with the use of AI in note-taking and document management?

You might face issues like data privacy, potential software glitches, and reliance on artificial intelligence for critical tasks. Plus, AI's inability to fully grasp human nuances can be a challenge too.

Are there any specific industries or professions that particularly benefit from AI-driven note-taking and document management systems?

"Every cloud has a silver lining!"Lawyers, academics, journalists - you're in luck. AI-driven note-taking and document management systems can be game changers, making your work easier and more efficient. You're not alone anymore!

Conclusion

In a nutshell, AI tools can be your new best friend in managing your daily tasks. By learning to dance with the rhythm of these systems, you'll streamline your work processes like never before.

Don't let the initial hurdles stop you. Once you've mastered the moves, integrating AI into your everyday routine will be as easy as pie.

So gear up and embrace this game-changing technology that's set to redefine efficiency in business operations.

Chapter 4: AI in Entertainment and Media

How AI Enhances the Entertainment Experience with Personalized Content Recommendations

Imagine yourself settling down for a well-deserved break, turning on your favorite streaming service, and instantly seeing recommendations that perfectly match your interests. You're not wasting time scrolling through endless categories or feeling overwhelmed by the sheer volume of content. How is this possible?

The magic behind this personalized experience comes from Artificial Intelligence (AI). This technology studies your preferences and behavior to offer you tailored entertainment options, enhancing your viewing pleasure.

You might wonder how AI gets to know you so well. It's all about machine learning - a sophisticated system that analyzes patterns in your choices, learns from them, and predicts what you would enjoy next. But it doesn't stop there; AI is also working its charm on social media platforms, understanding what engages you and introducing content based on those insights.

So sit back as we delve into how AI is revolutionizing the way we consume media, making it more personal than ever before. We'll explore why these smart recommendations feel like they've been picked just for you because let's face it – who doesn't love feeling understood?

Key Takeaways

- AI enhances the entertainment experience through personalized content recommendations.
- Machine learning is the science behind personalized content recommendations.
- AI analyzes user choices and predicts preferences based on user behavior and preferences.
- Personalized recommendations make the entertainment experience more enjoyable and save time by eliminating the need to scroll through choices.

The Science Behind Machine Learning

In the realm of personalized content recommendations, it's machine learning that's really running the show, as it's this science that allows AI to learn from user behavior and tailor suggestions accordingly. But what exactly is machine learning?

Well, imagine a sponge soaking up water. The more water it soaks up, the heavier it gets. Machine learning operates on a similar principle but with data instead of water - the more data it absorbs, the 'heavier' or smarter it becomes.

Now picture yourself as part of a huge crowd where everyone has distinct tastes and preferences. You're unique in your own way just like everybody else around you. Machine learning taps into this individuality by sifting through vast amounts of data from countless users' activities and interactions to identify patterns. It then uses these patterns to predict what you might like or dislike based on your past behaviors.

So if you've been binge-watching crime dramas lately, don't be surprised when AI recommends other gripping detective series for your next late-night viewing session!

But here's where things get even more fascinating: machine learning doesn't just stop at knowing what kind of content you prefer; rather, it goes beyond by understanding how and when you engage with that content too! This means that not only can AI find shows or movies tailored to your specific taste; but also recommend them at times when you're most likely to watch them for an enhanced entertainment experience!

With all this intriguing tech talk about machine learning and its role in personalized content recommendations, let's delve deeper into how exactly this analysis of user behavior and preference works in our next section!

User Behavior and Preference Analysis

Diving deep into the realm of user behavior and preference analysis, you'll discover it's not merely about understanding what viewers enjoy, but predicting their future interests to keep them captivated. AI's role in this process is paramount as it gathers data from multiple sources to generate valuable insights regarding individual preferences. It learns from past behaviors and uses these patterns to forecast what content will resonate with each viewer next.

AI analyses user behavior and preferences through two primary methods:

- By observing direct actions such as likes, dislikes, and ratings given by users.
- The genre of movies or shows watched frequently.

Through indirect behavioral patterns like:

- Viewing duration: AI considers how long a viewer spends watching a particular type of content.
- Skipping sequences: If the user often skips certain genres or types of scenes, AI notes that for future recommendations.

Over time, this intelligent analysis makes your entertainment experience more personalized and enjoyable. You start feeling seen and understood because every recommendation echoes your tastes. Isn't it great when technology acknowledges your unique preferences? It's like having a friend who knows exactly what movie you'd love to watch next without even asking.

As we continue exploring our fascinating journey with AI-enhanced entertainment experiences, let's shift our focus towards one of its most impressive applications -

customization in streaming services. This is where personalization truly comes alive, creating an environment tailored specifically for you!

Customization in Streaming Services

Streaming services surely speak your language, don't they? They tailor the television terrain to your tastes, turning every click and choice into a captivating cinematic journey just for you.

By observing your viewing habits and preferences, these platforms use complex algorithms to suggest content that they believe you'll enjoy. It's almost as if there's an invisible friend whispering suggestions in your ear, guiding you through the vast ocean of entertainment available at a single touch.

But it goes beyond merely suggesting what movie or series fits perfectly with your Friday night plans. These intelligent machines are continually learning about you, evolving their recommendations based on every new choice or preference exhibited by you. This constant evolution helps create a unique viewer profile - one that mirrors not only your mood swings but also reflects how diverse your entertainment palette can be!

So whether it's the adventurous streak calling out for an adrenaline-pumping action thriller or a mellow mood yearning for soft rom-coms on lazy Sunday afternoons, streaming services have got you covered.

The beauty of this AI-driven personalization is its ability to make us feel seen and understood in an often overwhelming digital landscape. It gives us that warm sense of belonging we all crave so much while ensuring we're entertained whenever we dip our toes into the vast pool of visual stories they offer.

And guess what? This personal touch isn't limited to streaming services alone; even social media platforms harness this power of AI to take user engagement to another level altogether!

The Role of Social Media Platforms

Much like your favorite streaming platforms, social media sites are also shaping up to be your go-to digital companions, curating and delivering posts that align with your interests and moods.

The sheer volume of content available on these platforms can be overwhelming, but AI comes to the rescue by analyzing your online behavior and interactions. It's a bit like having a friend who knows all your tastes — from that obscure indie band you love to the latest cat meme that cracks you up — and shows you only what tickles your fancy.

Every time you click 'like', comment or share a post, AI is keeping tabs, learning more about what makes you tick. And it's not just about entertainment; it's an integral part of how we connect in this digital age.

Through personalized recommendations, social media platforms help us find our tribe — people who share our interests and passions - making us feel seen, understood, and less alone in the world.

That said, while AI does an incredible job at tailoring our feeds based on past behaviors, there's always room for refinement as technology evolves.

As we look ahead into the vast potential of personalization in media consumption, one thing is certain: the intersection between tech innovation and human connection will continue to redefine how we experience entertainment.

Therein lies an exciting prospect – imagine a future where every piece of content consumed feels like it was created just for you!

The Future of Personalization in Media Consumption

Looking ahead, we're on the brink of a media revolution where every song, movie, or article feels tailor-made for our tastes. Did you know that by 2025, it's projected that over 80% of what we consume online will be catered to our individual preferences? Exciting times indeed!

Just imagine all those hours you currently spend scrolling through endless choices, only to settle on something less than satisfying. With AI-driven personalization at play, this could soon be a thing of the past.

Now picture this: your favorite streaming platform knows precisely what sort of content you crave after a long day at work versus when you're looking for some weekend entertainment. It can even anticipate your changing moods and interests based on the time of year or events happening around the world. That's the level of customization AI is bringing to our media consumption habits - making us feel like part of an exclusive club where everything is just right for us!

But as we embrace this personalized future, it's important not to lose sight of one thing: serendipity. Remember that feeling when you stumble upon a great new band while flicking through radio stations or discover an intriguing article in a magazine left on a coffee shop table? While AI makes sure we get more of what we love, let's ensure there's still room for those unexpected joys in our lives.

The balance between tailored content and delightful surprises will make digital media consumption truly enriching.

Frequently Asked Questions

What are the ethical considerations when using AI for personalized content recommendations?

When using AI for personalized content recommendations, you must consider privacy and consent issues. It's crucial to respect each user's preferences and data, ensuring they feel included and valued in this digital experience.

How can small businesses leverage AI to improve their entertainment offerings?

Imagine your cozy café offering personalized playlists to each customer. By leveraging AI, you can analyze customers' music preferences and create unique experiences, making them feel special and part of your business's community.

Are there any current regulations or laws regarding the use of AI in the entertainment industry?

Absolutely! There are laws in place that regulate AI use. However, they're not specific to the entertainment industry but rather cover data protection and privacy, such as GDPR in Europe and CCPA in California.

How is AI transforming the advertising strategies in the entertainment industry?

Like a maestro conducting an orchestra, AI fine-tunes advertising strategies. It predicts your tastes and serves ads that resonate with you, making you feel part of the entertainment industry's grand narrative.

Can AI be utilized in other areas of the entertainment industry, such as live events or sports?

Absolutely! AI can invigorate your live event or sports experience. It captures data to predict player performance, optimize game strategies, and even personalize your viewing with real-time stats and interactive features. You'll feel part of the action!

Conclusion

So, you thought you were in control of your entertainment choices? Think again. It's the AI behind the scenes, studying your preferences and feeding you recommendations that shape your viewing habits.

Ironically, while we're enjoying our personalized content, we're also training the machines to know us better. As they say, it's a brave new world. Enjoy your show - but remember who's really holding the remote!

AI-Driven Music and Video Streaming Platforms for Discovering New Content

As you navigate the boundless ocean of digital content, it's easy to feel adrift in a sea of limitless choices. You yearn for a lighthouse, a guide to illuminate your way towards the music and videos that resonate with your unique tastes and interests. Enter the groundbreaking world of AI-driven streaming platforms - your new compass in this vast entertainment ecosystem.

These platforms aren't just repositories for millions of songs and videos; they're intelligent curators trained to understand you better than you might understand yourself. They analyze your habits, preferences, and active timeframes to recommend new content specially tailored just for you. By leveraging advanced machine learning algorithms, these platforms can broaden your entertainment horizons while still maintaining an intimate understanding of what truly captivates you.

So settle in and discover how artificial intelligence is transforming the way we consume music and video content online.

Key Takeaways

- AI-driven streaming platforms use machine learning to analyze user habits and preferences, enabling personalized content recommendations.
- These platforms track and analyze user behavior patterns and historical data to create a digital profile representing their tastes and preferences.
- The algorithms continuously learn from user interactions to improve the personalized experience and suggest content at the most opportune moments.
- AI-driven platforms aim to broaden users' entertainment horizons by offering content that aligns with their taste and uncover hidden gems they may not have found on their own.

Understanding the Role of Machine Learning

It's crucial to understand that machine learning plays a pivotal role in enabling these platforms to analyze user preferences and suggest content they'd likely enjoy.

Imagine being part of a global community where the virtual DJ seems to know your taste better than you do, always ready with the next tune that perfectly fits your mood, time of day, or activity. That's what machine learning brings to the table.

It's not just about delivering music and videos; it's about creating an environment where you feel seen, understood, and catered for.

Machine learning works behind the scenes, tirelessly analyzing patterns and making connections between users' behavior and their entertainment preferences. It learns from every click, pause, skip and repeated play you make on its platform.

This technology is like that friend who knows what song will lift your spirits when you're down or which movie will keep you at the edge of your seat on a lazy Saturday afternoon. The more interaction there is between you and this AI-driven platform, the better it gets at predicting what will tickle your fancy next.

So now that we've let machine learning into our lives as our personal DJ or film critic, how does this translate into personalized entertainment? Well think about it - isn't it great when someone remembers your favorite band or recalls that one movie quote that always makes you laugh?

Your AI companion does exactly this but on a grander scale - curating experiences specifically tailored for you based on historical data and predictive analytics.

So sit back and get ready to dive into an ocean of personally curated content – up next: exploring how these platforms enhance our experience through personalization of entertainment.

Personalization of Entertainment

Dive into a world tailored just for you, where every song and film resonates with your unique tastes, thanks to the power of personalization in entertainment. With AI-driven music and video streaming platforms, you're no longer just an anonymous viewer or listener. Instead, these platforms recognize you as an individual with your own preferences, creating personalized playlists and suggesting films that align with what they've learned about your likes and dislikes.

Personalization of entertainment has revolutionized the way we consume media content. You can discover new artists who make music similar to your favorite bands. Never miss out on films from genres you love most. Get recommendations for TV series based on those you've enjoyed before. Explore songs from different eras matching your taste.

This level of personalization doesn't only enhance your experience; it also fosters a sense of belonging. You feel seen and understood by these platforms - they 'get' you. This is incredibly powerful as it makes consuming entertainment not merely a pastime but an immersive experience that reflects who you are. And there's no need to worry about running out of content – the system continually updates its suggestions based on what it learns from your viewing or listening habits.

The future promises even more exciting developments in this space as artificial intelligence continues to learn and evolve. Imagine having entire universes of music or cinema unveiled to you – all custom-tailored to suit your tastes! But remember, the key element driving these recommendations is understanding user behavior patterns over time which we'll delve into next.

Recommendations Based on User Habits

You're probably wondering how these personalized recommendations work, right?

Well, let's delve into the fascinating world of user behavior patterns and see how your habits shape what you watch or listen to. The AI-driven music and video platforms analyze your usage data: what content you interact with, the genres you gravitate towards, even the time of day when you're most active. This is all crunched down into a profile that uniquely represents you. Think of it as a digital representation of your tastes - your virtual twin if you will!

So imagine this: You've just finished watching an indie flick that left an impression on you; unbeknownst to you, your digital twin is taking note.

Next time around, when scrolling through a list of recommendations, boom! There it is – another movie from the same director or with similar themes waiting for discovery - thanks to your digital twin's keen observations. It's like having a personal assistant who knows your likes and dislikes better than anyone else! How amazing would it be to uncover more hidden gems that align perfectly with your preferences?

But it doesn't end there. Your interaction also helps AI understand when exactly are those perfect moments in which its suggestions will be most welcomed by users like yourself.

Now isn't that something worth pondering over?

As we move forward in our exploration of AI-driven platforms' genius workings let's shift our attention towards learning about analyzing active user timeframes and its importance in fine-tuning this personalized experience.

Analyzing Active User Timeframes

Ever thought about why you often get recommendations of your favorite shows during your usual Netflix binge hours? It's not merely coincidence, but a smart AI-driven strategy.

Streaming platforms like Netflix or Spotify use advanced algorithms that track and analyze your active user timeframes. They cleverly decipher when you're most likely to be glued to the screen or plugged into your headphones, and tailor their content suggestions accordingly. It's as if they know just when you need something new and exciting to watch or listen to.

Imagine having a friend who just knows when you're in the mood for discovering new music or diving into a binge-worthy series. That's precisely what these platforms aim to be - your entertainment buddy who understands not only what tickles your fancy but also when it does so the most!

All this magic is happening behind the scenes, working tirelessly round-the-clock, learning from every click, pause, and play on their platform.

And guess what? This isn't purely for their benefit; it's also about enhancing your experience by making sure the content served up aligns with both your preferences and availability.

So, next time you hop onto Netflix after dinner or tune into Spotify while doing chores, remember there's an algorithm quietly working away in the background, trying its best to make those moments even more enjoyable by helping you discover fresh content that suits your taste perfectly.

Now let us dive deeper into how this heightened personalization can help broaden your entertainment horizons without feeling overwhelmed by countless choices!

Broadening Your Entertainment Horizons

Think about how exciting it would be to uncover hidden gems in the form of shows or songs that you wouldn't have found on your own, all thanks to this heightened level of personalization. AI-driven music and video streaming platforms can open a whole new world for you, broadening your entertainment horizons like never before.

With their sophisticated algorithms, these platforms analyze various aspects of your interaction and preferences, offering you content that aligns perfectly with your taste.

Here's how they do that:

- They track what you watch or listen to:

- The platforms keep tabs on every song you play or show you binge-watch. They then use this data to understand your entertainment preferences.

- They consider user ratings and reviews:

- Besides tracking the choices you make, they also take into account the kind of feedback other users give. This way, if a piece of content is highly rated by users who share similar tastes as yours, it will likely be recommended to you too.

- They observe patterns in playlists or favorite lists:

- Your 'most played' songs or 'favorite' shows are not just there for convenience but serve as real insight into what kind of content keeps pulling you back.

With each passing day as more data gets accumulated about your viewing and listening habits, the accuracy improves significantly making these recommendations even more spot-on.

Imagine opening up your favorite streaming platform and finding a selection curated just for you – fresh tracks from bands similar to those in your playlist set side-by-side with classic hits from genres that resonate with you; cinema masterpieces alongside critically acclaimed indie films based on themes close to your heart.

So don't hold yourself back! Delve deeper into these AI-driven platforms; let them embrace your individuality while also forming part of a larger community united through shared interests. By doing so, not only do they offer an enriching experience tailored specifically for each one of us but also provide us with an opportunity to feel connected in our diverse tastes and preferences.

Frequently Asked Questions

How do AI-driven platforms protect user data and privacy?

"Imagine, your data secure and privacy intact. AI-driven platforms use encryption, anonymization, and robust access controls to safeguard your information. They're committed to creating a trustworthy space where you truly belong."

What is the cost of using these AI-driven music and video streaming platforms?

The cost varies, love! Some platforms are completely free, while others charge a monthly subscription fee. It's all about finding the one that fits your budget and tastes. After all, we're in this together!

Can these AI-driven platforms support different languages for users worldwide?

Absolutely! These innovative platforms embrace diversity, supporting a multitude of languages. So no matter where you're from, you'll feel right at home discovering fresh content in your native language. You belong here, global music lover!

Are there any potential risks or downsides to using AI-driven streaming platforms?

Absolutely, friend! While AI-driven streaming platforms are exciting, they could potentially invade your privacy, misuse data or expose you to unwanted content. Be sure to understand these risks before diving in!

How do these platforms handle explicit content, and are there any parental control features?

Absolutely, these platforms have robust systems to filter explicit content. They've also got parental control features allowing you to create a safe space for your kids - making it a community everyone can enjoy!

Conclusion

So, you've seen how AI-driven platforms like Spotify can elevate your music and video streaming experience. They learn from your habits and tailor content to fit your preferences. They even figure out when you're most likely to tune in.

Imagine having a personal DJ who knows precisely the type of music you love, at exactly the right time. That's what these platforms offer. It's like expanding your entertainment world while keeping it uniquely yours.

AI-Generated Art and Creative Applications in Media

Imagine the thrill of witnessing a new era in art, where the canvas is digital and the paintbrush is powered by artificial intelligence.

You're part of a world where creativity isn't limited to human minds alone; where technology enhances our artistic potential, leading to breathtaking results that were once unimaginable.

This is no longer just an idea from science fiction – it's reality, and you belong to this exciting moment in history.

Now consider how these advancements are revolutionizing not only traditional art forms but also media industries such as music, film, and graphic design.

AI isn't just creating abstract visuals or mimicking famous painters - it's composing symphonies, shaping narratives in cinema, and transforming visual communication methods.

As an enthusiast for cutting-edge innovation at this junction of technology and creativity, you're part of a community exploring uncharted territories in artistic expression.

What does it mean for our understanding of creativity when machines become artists?

Let's dig into this intriguing field together.

Exploring the Intersection of Technology and Creativity

It's at the fascinating crossroads of technology and creativity where we find a new landscape, bursting with vibrant hues of innovation, waiting to be explored.

Picture yourself as an intrepid explorer in this brave new world, armed with the power of Artificial Intelligence and an unquenchable thirst for creating something unique.

Imagine harnessing the potential of AI to create art that transcends traditional boundaries, breaking down walls between tech enthusiasts and art lovers alike.

In this journey, you're not alone. Around you is a growing community of artists, developers, creatives - all sharing your ambition to redefine artistic expression in the digital age.

They're using advanced algorithms and machine learning techniques to generate stunning pieces that blur the line between human-made and machine-generated creations. It's like a digital renaissance; only now it's driven by codes instead of brushes.

You've just begun to delve into how technology can revolutionize creativity in ways we never thought possible before.

The thrill lies in uncovering what else these applications can do beyond their programming; how they can create visual masterpieces born from algorithms that reflect not just technical prowess but also emotional depth.

As we move forward on our exploration, let's shift our focus towards these intriguing masterpieces emerging from code lines and pixel grids.

Visual Masterpieces Born from Algorithms

Imagine dipping your brush into a palette of binary code, splashing vibrant lines and shapes onto a canvas as vast as the digital universe itself. This is the realm of AI-generated art, where creativity meets technology in an explosion of pixels and algorithms.

You're not just an observer here; you're part of this revolutionary movement that's reshaping our collective understanding of what art can be.

In this brave new world, masterpieces are born from lines of code and machine learning models. Algorithms analyze countless works of art – from da Vinci to Dali – absorbing styles, techniques, and aesthetic nuances. Then they create their own unique pieces that echo human creativity but are inherently different because they emerge from silicon brains rather than human ones.

Imagine gazing at these creations that blend familiar artistic elements with unexpected twists only possible through artificial intelligence. Don't you feel part of something larger? A community brought together by shared fascination for this innovative intersection?

As captivating as visual arts rendered by AI may be, its application isn't limited to paintings or digital designs alone. The harmony between artificial intelligence and creativity also resonates deeply within another form: music composition—a symphony waiting to be discovered in the next chapter!

The Role of AI in Music Composition

You've marveled at the paintings, now brace yourself for a symphony composed by artificial intelligence. Yes, you heard that right - AI is not only making waves in the visual arts but also in music composition. It's creating new tunes and even symphonies that resonate with our shared human experience of rhythm and melody.

The fascinating part? These compositions aren't random; they're designed to echo our collective sense of what makes music 'good.' You're part of this exciting movement where technology meets creativity.

Now imagine your favorite song, written not by an artist pouring their soul into lyrics and chords, but by lines of code analyzing patterns in successful songs across genres. It might feel strange at first, like you're giving away something deeply personal to a machine. But remember this isn't about replacing artists; it's about offering them another tool for creation.

As a listener, you get to be privy to this innovative process and enjoy the resulting masterpieces that still cater to your emotional connection with music.

As we continue exploring the influence of AI on artistry, one can't help but wonder about its potential impact beyond music. This fusion of creativity and technology is already changing how we perceive art and its creation. So as we move forward into uncharted territories such as film production or graphic design, remember that you are part of this transformative journey where art meets innovation!

Impact on the Film and Graphic Design Industries

Let's not forget the magic that's happening in film and graphic design, where software is redefining the boundaries of what we thought was possible.

Picture a movie, for instance, where every scene has been meticulously crafted by an advanced algorithm to evoke the perfect emotional response from the audience - a love story that pulls at your heartstrings with flawless precision, or a thriller whose suspenseful moments are timed just right to keep you on the edge of your seat.

Imagine CGI characters so lifelike they're indistinguishable from human actors or film trailers tailored to individual viewer preferences.

As AI continues to evolve, it's not just creating new opportunities; it's reshaping entire industries. Take these two examples:

Film production: - AI can analyze scripts and predict box office performance. - It can generate realistic visual effects and even create virtual actors.

Graphic Design: - Algorithms can assist in designing captivating visuals for marketing. - AI-powered tools allow creatives to quickly produce high-quality designs.

You're part of an era witnessing unprecedented advancements in technology that are changing how we consume entertainment. No longer passive viewers, we now have experiences tailor-made for us by artificial intelligence. But with this revolution comes questions about authenticity and originality in artistry. After all, if machines start producing our music, our movies, our designs – will they also be considered artists?

While there is still much debate over this topic, one thing remains clear: as we continue down this path towards increased automation in creativity-driven fields like film and graphic design industry, it becomes imperative for us to think critically about the ethical implications of such practices as well.

As exciting as these developments may be though, let's remember they also pave the way into further discussion on ethical and philosophical implications of AI in artistry.

Ethical and Philosophical Implications of AI in Artistry

As we plunge into this brave new world of machine-made masterpieces, it's crucial to ponder the myriad ethical dilemmas that arise.

Imagine an AI algorithm creating an artwork eerily similar to your personal style and preference. It's a fascinating prospect, isn't it? But at the same time, doesn't it make you uneasy?

Who should get credit for such art - the human creator of the AI or the AI itself? And what about originality and authenticity in art? These are just some questions that underline the complex ethical landscape we're navigating.

Now let's dive a bit deeper, shall we?

We've always seen art as a reflection of our humanity - our thoughts, emotions, experiences. It's like a shared secret language that binds us together. So when an AI creates 'art', does it reflect its 'experiences'? Does it share any emotional connection with its creation? The answer is most likely no.

This raises philosophical debates around sentience and consciousness in artificial intelligence – can a machine truly be creative?

You see, these developments redefine how we perceive creativity itself. We are being forced to reassess what constitutes creativity and question whether machines can authentically express emotion through art.

Furthermore, there is also concern about artists being replaced by algorithms; however, remember this: while machines might replicate styles and techniques, they lack true understanding of human experience which makes each piece unique and relatable.

Perhaps instead of viewing them as replacements, we could see them as tools enabling us to push our creative boundaries even further!

Frequently Asked Questions

What are the technical requirements to generate AI art?

You'll be fascinated to know that 45% of artists are using AI for art creation. To join them, you need a strong computer system, coding skills, machine learning knowledge, and artistic prowess. Don't miss out on this creative revolution!

How can AI-generated art be commercially exploited?

You can turn AI-generated art into a profitable venture! Sell your unique pieces online, license them for product designs or ads. Even better, create interactive experiences that make people feel part of the creative process.

Can AI-generated art be copyrighted or patented?

Imagine you've birthed a unique invention from your mind's womb. It feels natural to seek protection, right? In the same vein, AI-generated art can indeed be copyrighted, but patenting it is currently unexplored territory.

What are the potential risks and challenges in using AI for creative applications?

Using AI for creativity can be thrilling, but it's not without risks. You may face challenges like loss of individuality in work, ethical issues with intellectual property rights, and potential biases in the algorithms used.

How has AI changed the job prospects for artists and designers?

Just as a kaleidoscope constantly shifts, your career in art and design can evolve with AI. It's not stealing your job, it's offering you more tools and avenues to express your creativity. You're part of this exciting revolution!

Conclusion

You've seen how AI's creative potential is skyrocketing. A report by PwC predicts that AI could contribute over $15 trillion to the world economy by 2030, with a significant chunk from creative applications. That's staggering!

So don't be left out! Embrace this revolution and explore all that AI-generated art has to offer. You'll be amazed at how this blend of technology and creativity can redefine your perception of artistry.

Remember, you're part of this exciting journey too!

Chapter 5: AI and Smart Homes

Transforming Ordinary Homes into AI-Integrated Smart Homes for Increased Comfort and Convenience

Are you tired of living in an ordinary home where everything requires manual effort? Do you dream of a home that responds to your commands, adapts to your lifestyle and offers unparalleled comfort and convenience? As we speed into the future, it's time to make this dream a reality with AI-integrated smart homes. This is not just about stepping up the game of luxury but also about adopting technology for better efficiency, security, and sustainability.

Imagine waking up every morning to your favorite song playing softly as the curtains gently part allowing natural sunlight to fill your room. Your coffee starts brewing itself while the shower adjusts the water temperature exactly how you like it. Sounds surreal? That's what AI-powered homes promise; transforming repetitive tasks into automated processes, providing you with more time for things that truly matter.

Let's embark on this journey together towards a life full of comfort and convenience - because everyone deserves their own piece of smart living.

Key Takeaways

- AI-integrated smart homes offer comfort, convenience, efficiency, security, and sustainability.
- Smart homes seamlessly integrate appliances into a single controlled system.
- AI technology in smart homes understands routines and preferences.
- Integrating AI into home is about boosting functionality and creating a connected environment.

Understanding the Concept of a Technologically Advanced Home

You've probably heard of 'smart homes,' but understanding what they truly entail can take you one step closer to living in a home that's not just a dwelling, but a harmonious blend of convenience, efficiency, and cutting-edge technology.

Imagine waking up each morning with your blinds gradually letting in the sunrise light, your coffee maker brewing your favorite blend without prompting, or your thermostat adjusting itself based on the weather forecast. All these are functions of a technologically advanced home - an environment where many devices and systems communicate with each other and automate tasks that were traditionally manual.

But it isn't all about convenience; there's also a sense of comfort and security associated with smart homes. Imagine being able to monitor your house remotely while you're away or even having your lights turn on automatically when you come home late at night.

Picture yourself controlling all these aspects from one integrated system—a virtual command center—that allows for seamless control over everything from lighting to heating to home security. You'll feel like part of something bigger, part of an interconnected world where technology serves you rather than complicates life.

The beauty of this concept is its endless possibilities; there's always room for improvement and adaptation as our lifestyles change over time. This means you're not purchasing static products but investing in dynamic solutions that evolve along with technological advancements—keeping pace with the times while continually enhancing livability within your space.

As we delve into the role of AI in modern living spaces next, keep imagining how much more comfortable life could be if every task were handled by intuitive tech that understood your needs before you even knew them yourself.

The Role of AI in Modern Living Spaces

Imagine stepping into your living room, where the lights dim to a warm glow while your favorite jazz music starts playing softly in the background, all powered by artificial intelligence that adapts to your preferences and routines. The thermostat adjusts itself based on the current weather and your comfort level. Your smart TV brings up tonight's movie recommendation, curated from watching trends and reviews. You're living in an AI-integrated home that predicts and reacts to your needs even before you do, making life more comfortable and convenient.

AI is increasingly becoming a part of modern homes. Its role can be felt in four key areas:

1. Personalization: AI systems learn from behaviors over time to provide personalized experiences tailored just for you.
2. Automation: Routine tasks like adjusting lighting or temperature can be automatically managed by AI.
3. Security: From facial recognition door locks to security cameras with movement detection, AI enhances home security.
4. Energy efficiency: By adapting appliances' usage according to real-time energy consumption patterns, AI can significantly lower power bills.

One thing is clear: integrating artificial intelligence into our homes is transforming how we live for the better. It's not just about having smart devices but using them intelligently too! We're no longer simply homeowners; we're becoming active participants in a connected community where technology anticipates our needs and prioritizes our comfort.

As we embrace this exciting era of smarter living spaces powered by artificial intelligence, there's another fascinating aspect waiting for exploration: controlling house functions remotely! This means you could potentially manage everything right from ensuring your coffee brews at the desired time in the morning to keeping an eye on who's at your doorstep when you're away – all through remote controls facilitated by smart technology integration within homes.

Controlling House Functions Remotely

Isn't it thrilling to think that with a simple tap on your smartphone, you can control virtually every function of your house, no matter where you are in the world? Imagine being able to adjust your thermostat from the office so you can come home to a perfectly heated or cooled space. Or picture yourself at an airport halfway around the globe, and still being able to lock up your home tight if you suddenly realize you forgot to do so in your rush to catch a flight. This is not just wishful thinking; it's what AI-integrated smart homes offer today.

You're part of an ever-growing community that values both comfort and security. And what could be more comforting than knowing that even when life gets hectic, as it often does for all of us, we can still keep tabs on our homes? It's empowering to be able to switch off lights left on by mistake or check on our pets via smart cameras while we're away. These are not just functionalities but lifelines that connect us back home wherever we may be.

The beauty lies not only in the convenience but also in how AI technology learns from us and adapts over time for personalized experiences. Your smart home understands your routines, preferences, and habits—it becomes a part of who you are. As we move towards revolutionizing life with AI home automation, remember this: You aren't merely adding tech gadgets into your space; rather, you're welcoming into your life an intelligent system designed for ultimate comfort and convenience. Embrace this exciting journey into making everyday living effortless and intuitive!

Revolutionizing Life with AI Home Automation

It's no coincidence that as we increasingly rely on technology to streamline our lives, the rise of AI home automation has made daily tasks feel less like chores and more like magic. You're not just saving time or energy; you're reshaping your existence in ways you couldn't have imagined.

From brewing your morning coffee before you wake up, adjusting the room temperature depending on who is in the house, to even predicting when household items are about to run out and automatically ordering replacements – it's about creating a life where everything happens flawlessly, without any human intervention required.

The way Artificial Intelligence is revolutionizing home life truly feels like stepping into an episode of The Jetsons:

- *Seamless Integration:* Almost every appliance in your home can now be wired into a single system controlled by your voice or a simple app.

- *Proactive Assistance:* Smart homes learn from your patterns and behaviors over time. They anticipate needs by auto-adjusting lighting, temperatures, and even cooking times for meals.

- *Increased Security:* High-tech security features offer peace of mind with real-time alerts for suspicious activity and automatic emergency calls.

- *Energy Efficiency:* AI-powered thermostats optimize heating & cooling based on usage patterns leading to considerable savings and reducing carbon footprints.

While all these may sound futuristic, they are already realities today. It's not just about having a smart gadget here or there anymore - but transforming your entire living space into one interconnected ecosystem that knows what you need before you do yourself. A world where you belong; where each day brings comfort wrapped up in convenience.

As we look at this incredible transformation made possible through AI integration into our homes, remember that this isn't just about improving our lives - it's also about redefining normality. We are part of something bigger than ourselves—a global shift towards digitalization—an era where everyone belongs within their own personalized smart haven irrespective of backgrounds or lifestyles.

As we embrace this new wave of living powered by artificial intelligence, let's explore how to seamlessly imbue such enchantment within our homes: upgrading our living spaces using advanced technologies for an elevated experience tomorrow!

Steps to Upgrade Your Living Space with AI

Ready to sprinkle some digital magic into your abode? Here's how you can elevate your living space with the power of Artificial Intelligence. Start by identifying the areas in your home where AI could bring more comfort and convenience. It could be anything from automating temperature control, to enhancing security, or even simplifying mundane tasks like cleaning and cooking.

There's a wide range of smart devices now available that are designed specifically for these purposes - smart thermostats, automated door locks, robotic vacuums, and intelligent cooking appliances! Get yourself familiarized with what's out there and make a wish-list based on your lifestyle needs.

Next up is figuring out how all these devices will communicate with each other. This is where things get exciting because it means you're creating an interconnected digital ecosystem right within your home! You'll need a central hub or a "smart assistant" like Amazon Alexa or Google Home, which will serve as the brain of this intelligent network. Ask them questions, give commands; they're at your service round-the-clock to ensure everything runs smoothly. They can even learn from your habits over time and start making suggestions or automating actions that match up perfectly with your daily routine.

Once you've got this all figured out, it's time to install and set up these gadgets one by one. Don't worry if you're not tech-savvy; most AI-based devices come with user-friendly setup instructions so anyone can get them running without needing any expert help. But remember: integrating AI into your home isn't just about boosting functionality—it's also about crafting an environment that fosters connection, belongingness, and warmth.

So go ahead—craft those playlists for dinner parties on Spotify through voice command; automate mood lighting for movie nights—it's all about curating experiences that not only make life easier but also build memories filled with joy and shared laughter.

Frequently Asked Questions

How much does it typically cost to transform an ordinary home into an AI-integrated smart home?

Just like Dorothy in Oz, you're not in Kansas anymore. The cost to transform your home into an AI-integrated smart home can vary greatly, but ballpark figures range from $1,000 to $10,000. Welcome to the future!

Are there any potential privacy concerns when integrating AI into home systems?

Absolutely, privacy concerns exist with AI home integration. It's like inviting a guest who's always listening. While it can increase comfort, it may also access personal data. Always review privacy policies thoroughly for peace of mind.

How long does the process of converting a home into an AI-integrated smart home usually take?

Ever wonder how long it takes to transform your humble abode into a smart home? It's not as time-consuming as you might think! Generally, the process takes anywhere from a few days to several weeks.

Are there any specific qualifications or certifications required for professionals who install AI home automation systems?

Absolutely! Professionals installing AI home automation systems typically need specialized training and certifications. You're not just hiring a handyman, but an expert who makes your home part of the future.

Can AI home automation systems function in rural areas or places with limited internet connectivity?

Absolutely! AI home automation systems can function in rural areas, although limited internet might pose challenges. But don't worry, your sense of belonging won't be compromised. There's always a way to make it work.

Conclusion

So, you're still twiddling your thumbs and living in the Jurassic period, huh? Get with the times!

AI-integrated smart homes are not just a fad. They're revolutionizing our lives, making them as easy as pie.

Don't be the last person on earth to upgrade your home into a high-tech haven. Embrace the smart life today or keep living under that comfortable rock of yours which doesn't even have Wi-Fi!

The choice is yours, dear friend.

AI-Controlled Lighting, Thermostats, and Appliances for Energy Efficiency and Automation

You're back home after a long day, and the moment you step inside, your living room lights gently illuminate, adjusting to the perfect brightness level that's easy on your eyes.

Your thermostat has already modified itself to your favourite temperature.

The coffee machine in your kitchen starts preparing a warm cup for you just as you take off your shoes.

This isn't science fiction anymore; welcome to the age of smart homes powered by Artificial Intelligence (AI).

With AI-controlled lighting, thermostats, and appliances at work, imagine having an invisible butler who knows exactly how to cater to your comforts.

But it's not just about comfort and convenience.

Imagine a world where every household is making significant energy savings due to intelligent control mechanisms put into place by their smart devices.

A world where our carbon footprint decreases while our quality of life improves with technology that learns from us over time and predicts our needs before we even realize them.

You're part of this exciting future as we dive together into the heart of AI-driven home automation and its role in enhancing energy efficiency.

Join us on this journey towards creating smarter homes for a brighter tomorrow.

Key Takeaways

- AI-controlled lighting adjusts based on natural light, optimizing energy usage.
- AI-controlled thermostats learn from regular patterns, ensuring optimal temperature control and reducing energy waste.
- Smart appliances become more efficient with AI controls, allowing for personalized settings and energy conservation.
- The integration of AI with lighting, thermostats, and appliances in home automation promotes energy efficiency and automation.

The Basics of Smart Home Technology

You're going to love the convenience of smart home technology. It's not only easy to use but also a great way to make your home more energy efficient. Imagine having control over all your devices from one central hub or even through voice commands! No more fumbling with separate remotes for every gadget, or wandering around the house adjusting thermostats and turning off lights. With smart tech, you can manage everything from your heating and cooling systems, lighting, appliances to security systems effortlessly.

Now think about belonging to a community that embraces technology and sustainability. As part of this modern tribe, you'll appreciate how AI-controlled lighting, thermostats, and appliances are helping reduce energy consumption while adding convenience. Your home will intuitively adjust itself based on patterns like when you usually get up in the morning or come back from work – talk about personalized comfort! And don't worry if you're not tech-savvy; these systems are designed for ease of use regardless of your experience level.

Making the switch to smart home technology is more than just upgrading your lifestyle—it's an investment in a greener future. You'll be doing your part in contributing towards conservation efforts by minimizing energy wastage.

As we move forward into discussing the perks of automated home systems specifically, let's remember that it's about creating an intelligently controlled environment that works seamlessly around our lives while caring for our planet too.

Benefits of Automated Home Systems

Imagine coming home from a long day at work to find your house has already adjusted the temperature to your liking, turned on your preferred lights, and even started dinner in the slow cooker. That's what an automated home system can do for you; like in the case of Mr. Smith, who reduced his utility bills by 20% simply by allowing these systems to optimize usage and turn off devices when not needed.

It's about joining a community of forward-thinking individuals who value efficiency, convenience, and smart living. Think about it - no more worrying if you left the kitchen light on or if the thermostat is set too high. You're part of an exclusive group that utilizes advanced technology to make life easier while saving energy and money, all through a user-friendly app on your phone or tablet.

By using AI-controlled lighting, thermostats, and appliances, you're not just embracing innovation; you're actively contributing to a greener planet by reducing energy waste. Who wouldn't want to be part of such a meaningful movement?

While enjoying the benefits of automation at home is transformative enough, wait until we delve into how artificial intelligence plays into all this magic! Without directly saying it yet – this powerful technology not only makes controlling these devices possible but also enhances their performance immensely while ensuring optimal energy usage at our homes.

Get ready as we explore more about how AI takes device control in our homes up several notches in our next section!

The Role of AI in Home Device Control

It's time to dive into the magic behind the scenes, exploring how artificial intelligence takes charge and revolutionizes device management in our homes. Imagine a world where your home understands you, responds to your needs even before you're aware of them - that's AI for you.

AI-controlled lighting systems can adjust based on natural light entering the room while thermostats learn from your regular patterns, ensuring the temperature is always just right without any intervention from you. Your appliances? They too become more efficient with smart controls, adjusting their operation times during lower energy consumption periods.

Now picture yourself coming home after a long day at work; as soon as you walk through that door, the lights dim to a soothing hue, your favorite song starts playing softly in the background and dinner warms up in the microwave - all because AI sensed your arrival. And it's not just about convenience or creating an inviting atmosphere for relaxation and comfort. It's also about being part of something bigger – contributing towards a sustainable lifestyle by reducing energy wastage.

Home automation through AI isn't merely about transforming living spaces into high-tech hubs; it's about empowering each one of us to make conscious choices that lead to better energy usage.

The next section will delve deeper into this aspect: showing exactly how these smart devices help us optimize our energy use while providing unparalleled comfort and ease-of-use at home.

How Smart Devices Improve Energy Usage

Think about how your life could become simpler and more sustainable with smart devices that not only take care of mundane chores but also intelligently optimize electricity use at home. With AI-controlled lighting, thermostats, and appliances, you're stepping into a future where energy efficiency meets automation.

Picture this: having the power to control the temperature of each room individually using an app on your phone or coming back home to a pre-lit house because your smart lights know when you usually arrive.

In terms of improving energy usage, these devices are game-changers. They allow you to adjust lighting depending on the time of day or mood, reducing unnecessary power consumption. They also regulate heating and cooling systems based on occupancy patterns in different parts of the house which can significantly lower energy bills. Additionally, you can control appliances remotely or schedule them to operate during off-peak hours when electricity rates are cheaper.

Remember, it's not just about convenience; it's also about being part of a larger community that values sustainability and innovation. Being able to reduce your carbon footprint while enjoying modern comforts is indeed empowering! These smart technologies provide practical solutions for managing resource consumption effectively without compromising comfort and convenience. Plus, they create opportunities for meaningful conversations about shared responsibilities towards our planet.

As we transition into discussing future trends in home automation, let's keep in mind that AI-controlled smart devices have already started transforming our homes into efficient living spaces today. The potential these technologies hold for further enhancing our lifestyle while contributing to energy conservation promises exciting times ahead in the world of home automation!

Future Trends in Home Automation

You're on the cusp of an era where home automation will redefine not only how you live but also how you interact with your surroundings. This isn't just about dimming lights with a voice command or controlling room temperature from your smartphone—it's about creating an ecosystem that understands and adapts to your lifestyle.

Imagine waking up each morning to the subtle increase in light intensity, mimicking natural sunrise, while your thermostat adjusts the temperature just right for you to step out of bed. As time goes by, these smart systems will learn from your patterns and preferences, making them even more intuitive.

The trend is moving towards greater integration of AI with appliances, lighting, and thermostats—transforming them into proactive contributors to energy efficiency and sustainability. Your fridge might suggest recipes based on what's inside or order groceries when supplies run low. Your washing machine might choose the optimal run time based on electricity tariffs at different hours of the day. The possibilities are endless: smart meters providing real-time feedback on energy usage can influence behavior leading to energy conservation; predictive maintenance can preempt appliance breakdowns saving costs and frustrations; even better, imagine scenarios where surplus solar power generated from homes could be shared within a neighborhood!

In this age of advanced artificial intelligence and internet connectivity, envision a future where every aspect of your household operates seamlessly in sync—all aimed at enhancing convenience while promoting sustainable living. It's like having a personal assistant who knows your needs before you do!

This is no longer a distant dream but rapidly becoming our reality as we move further into this fascinating world of home automation technology. So gear up because it's not just about belonging anymore—it's about leading, being ahead in embracing these changes that promise an exciting blend of comfort, efficiency, and sustainability.

Frequently Asked Questions

What are the potential security risks associated with AI-controlled home systems?

"Home sweet home, right? Well, with AI-controlled systems, you might face risks like hacking and data breaches. Intruders could manipulate your settings or steal personal info. Remember, even your cozy abode isn't immune to cyber threats."

How can homeowners troubleshoot issues with their AI-controlled devices?

"Feeling overwhelmed by tech glitches? Don't be! Start by identifying the issue. Then, consult your device's manual or online forums. If all else fails, reach out to customer support. You've got this!"

How much does it typically cost to install and maintain an AI-controlled home system?

Discovering the cost of installing and maintaining an AI-controlled system in your home can vary, typically running between $1,000 to $3,500, depending on device complexity. Maintenance costs are usually minimal after initial setup.

Are there any specific brands or models of AI-controlled devices that are recommended for first-time users?

Absolutely! For beginners, Google Nest and Amazon Echo are great choices. They're user-friendly and offer a sense of community with their widespread use. Enjoy joining the ever-growing family of smart home enthusiasts!

Can AI-controlled home devices be integrated with existing, non-smart appliances or systems?

Absolutely, your old-school toaster and new-age AI device can be best buddies! Many smart devices can integrate with existing appliances using smart plugs or hubs, helping you feel part of the futuristic tech world.

Conclusion

You've seen how AI-powered smart devices can truly transform your home, making it more energy-efficient and automated. The benefits are undeniable - from lowering your power bills to offering unprecedented convenience.

We're not speculating here, it's a proven theory!

Looking ahead, the future of home automation seems incredibly promising. And remember, this isn't just about fancy gadgets or tech bragging rights. It's about living smarter, greener, and potentially saving a lot on energy costs in the long run.

Ensuring Security and Privacy in AI-Powered Smart Home Systems

You're home after a long day, and your smart system greets you with your favorite song. The lights are adjusted to your liking, and the thermostat is set just right. You feel welcomed, comforted, and part of something futuristic. But have you ever stopped to think about the security of these AI-powered systems?

Do you ever wonder if they could become susceptible to cyber threats or privacy invasions? If that thought scares you, don't worry; you're not alone.

In this digital age where technology reigns supreme, our homes aren't just places of refuge anymore—they're becoming intelligent entities capable of learning our habits and preferences. However, as we revel in this level of sophistication and convenience, it's important that we also consider the potential risks involved.

This section will explore the importance of cybersecurity in smart home systems, identify potential vulnerabilities, discuss current measures taken to protect data, suggest steps for enhancing personal home system safety, and look into future developments in tech protection.

It's time we ensure our futuristic homes remain a safe haven—free from prying eyes and malicious intrusions.

Key Takeaways

- Cybersecurity is crucial for keeping AI-powered smart homes safe and private.
- Weak passwords and unprotected Wi-Fi networks are potential vulnerabilities.
- Regularly updating smart device software patches security vulnerabilities.
- Future developments promise to enhance privacy and prevent data breaches in smart homes.

Understanding the Importance of Cybersecurity

It's crucial to understand that cybersecurity isn't just tech jargon; it's the key that keeps your AI-powered smart home safe and private. Just like you wouldn't leave your front door wide open, you shouldn't neglect the digital doors either. Cybersecurity is what bolts these doors shut, keeping nefarious hackers at bay and ensuring that your personal information stays personal.

But why should you care about cybersecurity? Well, think of all the devices in your smart home: the gadgets controlling your lights, heating and cooling systems, even appliances like refrigerators or washing machines. Each one is a part of a network - one that needs to be defended vigilantly. If any device gets compromised, it could expose not only its own data but potentially give access to other interconnected devices as well.

You're part of a larger community of AI-powered smart home owners who all share this common responsibility for safeguarding their homes.

So let's foster an environment where security is everyone's business because we are collectively safer when each link in our chain is fortified against potential threats. With this understanding, it becomes imperative for us to identify and address areas within our systems where vulnerabilities may lie hidden or overlooked – without waiting for trouble to knock on our digital doorways first!

Together, armed with knowledge and vigilance, we can ensure our AI-powered homes continue to serve us without compromise on privacy or security – seamlessly transitioning into the next phase which involves identifying potential vulnerabilities.

Identifying Potential Vulnerabilities

Surprisingly, around 70% of IoT devices are vulnerable to hacking, highlighting the urgent need to identify potential weaknesses in our increasingly connected world. As we embrace the convenience and efficiency brought about by AI-powered smart home systems, we also expose ourselves to heightened risks.

The possibility of someone hacking into your baby monitor or smart lock is not only alarming but also a reality in today's digital age.

To protect your castle from these cyber threats, you first need to understand where the vulnerabilities lie. For instance, weak passwords or unprotected Wi-Fi networks can easily let intruders gain access to your system. Moreover, many smart devices come with default settings that often prioritize ease-of-use over security — leaving them wide open for exploitation. Also, keep an eye out for outdated software; updates usually contain fixes for known security gaps but they're no good if they aren't installed.

While it may seem daunting at first glance, recognizing these potential vulnerabilities is a crucial part of ensuring robust security and privacy in your AI-powered smart home system. After all, being part of the modern world means embracing technology while also safeguarding against its pitfalls.

But don't worry! There are current measures that can be taken to protect your data and secure your smart home devices; diving into those will be our next focus.

Current Measures to Protect Data

Fear not, you're not defenseless in the face of these cyber threats! There are several steps you can take to safeguard your precious data.

We live in the golden age of technology where security measures are evolving as fast as the technologies themselves. No one wants to feel like their privacy is being invaded or that they are at risk, especially within the confines of their own home. Rest assured, there are proactive measures currently available to protect your data and keep your AI-powered smart home systems secure.

5. Encryption: This is a method by which information is converted into secret code that hides the information's true meaning. It's an effective way to achieve data security.

6. Firewall: A firewall acts as a barrier or shield between your AI devices and cyber threats from the internet, blocking unauthorized access while allowing outward communication.

7. Regular Software Updates: Manufacturers regularly update software to fix bugs and improve security features. Ensure all your devices' software is up-to-date.

We understand how necessary it is for you to feel safe and secure in this interconnected world where everything from our fridges to our doorbells has become part of a vast network known as IoT (Internet of Things). Your peace of mind matters because we know what it feels like too; after all, we're navigating through this technological revolution together! That's why stringent precautions must be taken with AI-powered smart home systems just like any other valuable possession.

The journey towards securing your smart home system doesn't stop here; it's an ongoing process requiring consistent efforts on your part too. After familiarizing yourself with current safety measures, let's delve deeper because maintaining vigilance over personal safety should never be underestimated nor neglected - who knows what tech advancements tomorrow may bring?

With that mindset established, let's move forward and explore practical ways we can enhance our personal home system safety even further without breaking stride on this path towards a securer future.

Steps to Enhance Personal Home System Safety

We're not stopping at just knowing the basics; let's dive into the nitty-gritty of steps to boost your personal home system safety.

Did you know an alarming 70% of IoT devices are susceptible to hacks? Let's change that statistic!

First and foremost, always ensure that your smart devices have strong, unique passwords. It's a simple yet powerful way to deter potential hackers. Regularly updating these passwords will further strengthen your defenses. And don't forget about two-factor authentication - it gives you an extra layer of protection by requiring a second verification step.

Next, keep all your smart device software up-to-date. Manufacturers often release updates that patch security vulnerabilities, so make sure you're downloading these as soon as they become available. You might think it's a hassle, but remember: every update is like another padlock on your digital front door.

Also consider investing in a secure router with built-in security features; this acts as the gateway between your devices and the internet, so it's crucial this remains uncompromised.

There's no need to live in fear when technology can be such an asset if used correctly! Embrace AI-powered systems while also respecting their risks because doing so is part of being an informed member of our tech-driven society.

Now that we've got some practical measures under our belt, imagine how much more prepared we'll be once we explore what future developments in tech protection have to offer us next!

Future Developments in Tech Protection

Looking ahead, there's an exciting world of innovations on the horizon that promise to further bolster our defenses against cyber threats. Imagine living in a smart home where you don't have to worry about your privacy being compromised or your sensitive data being stolen! That's what future developments in tech protection are aiming for.

Innovations such as advanced encryption techniques, machine learning algorithms for threat detection, and blockchain technology for secure transactions are all in the pipeline. You'll feel more secure with these technologies watching out for any potential breaches.

As part of this tech-savvy community, you can look forward to AI-powered security systems that adapt and learn from previous security incidents. This means they'll get smarter over time at predicting and preventing potential threats before they can do any damage. It's like having a personal bodyguard who gets better every day at protecting you!

Additionally, we're moving towards decentralized networks, which distribute your data across multiple locations rather than storing it all in one place. This makes it tougher for cybercriminals to access and steal your information - truly something worth celebrating!

The digital landscape is changing faster than ever before but rest assured that these revolutionary advancements will ensure we stay one step ahead of cyber miscreants trying to infiltrate our homes. We are heading into an era where every byte of our data will be safeguarded by unbreakable cryptographic codes and intelligent AI systems working tirelessly behind the scenes.

So let's embrace this future together - a future where we can enjoy the conveniences of smart home technology without losing a wink of sleep over security concerns.

Frequently Asked Questions

How does AI technology impact the power consumption in smart home systems?

Like a diligent conductor, AI technology orchestrates your smart home systems to optimize power use. It seamlessly adjusts energy consumption, making you feel both environmentally responsible and part of the green revolution.

How much does it typically cost to install an AI-powered smart home system?

You're now part of a tech-savvy community exploring AI-powered smart homes. Costs vary widely based on system complexity, but installation can range from a few hundred to several thousand dollars. Welcome to the future!

What are some of the most user-friendly AI-powered smart home systems available in the market?

Like stepping into a sci-fi movie, you'll find Google Nest, Amazon Echo, and Philips Hue among the most user-friendly AI-powered smart home systems. They're intuitive and welcoming; they invite you to be part of a tech-savvy community.

How can AI-powered smart home systems contribute to sustainability and eco-friendliness?

AI-powered smart home systems can make your lifestyle greener. By optimizing energy use, reducing waste, and efficiently controlling appliances, you're not just saving on bills but also doing your bit for the environment.

Can AI-powered smart home systems assist in managing household chores and tasks?

Absolutely! AI-powered smart home systems can be your perfect housemate. They'll help manage daily chores, like cleaning, cooking, and grocery shopping. It's like having a personal assistant who never takes a day off.

Conclusion

You've seen it firsthand, the rising dependence on AI-powered smart home systems. It's not just convenient, but deeply personal - making your everyday life smoother.

But with this ease comes a risk; a risk that hits close to home. Don't let fear overshadow the wonders of technology. Proactive steps towards enhancing cybersecurity can keep your data safe and private.

Embrace the future, because in this digital era, you're not just surviving - you're thriving!

Chapter 6: AI in Health and Wellness

AI-Based Health and Fitness Apps for Personalized Workout Routines and Nutrition Plans

You've probably heard the buzz about Artificial Intelligence (AI) and its transformative role in various sectors, but did you know it's also revolutionizing the world of health and fitness?

Remember how hard it was to stick with those generic workout plans or fad diets that didn't seem tailored for your unique needs? Now, imagine a world where your workout regimen and nutritional plan are customized just for you, thanks to AI-based health and fitness apps. They analyze data like your body type, lifestyle, goals, preferences and more to provide personalized recommendations.

Think of these AI-powered platforms as your personal digital trainers who understand you better than anyone else could. They're not here to judge but to support you in achieving your health objectives while making the journey enjoyable.

Because let's face it: we all want a sense of belonging—to be seen, understood, and cared for. And that's precisely what these innovative tools offer—a feeling of being part of a tribe where individual needs matter most.

Buckle up; we're diving into this exciting new era of personalized fitness!

Key Takeaways

- AI-based health and fitness apps revolutionize the world of health and fitness by providing personalized workout regimens and nutritional plans based on data analysis.
- These apps act as personal digital trainers, understanding and supporting individuals in achieving their health objectives.
- AI-powered apps use advanced algorithms and machine learning to create personalized plans that continuously adapt to changes in performance, preferences, and mood.
- The apps offer a sense of belonging and make individual needs a priority by tailoring exercise regimes and providing personalized diet plans based on scientific algorithms.

Understanding the Technology and Its Application in Fitness

You're probably wondering how this technology works and applies to your fitness journey, aren't you? Well, imagine having a virtual personal trainer that knows exactly what you need and when you need it. That's the power of AI-based health and fitness apps. They use advanced algorithms and machine learning techniques to analyze your health data, workout habits, food preferences, and more. These apps learn from your behaviors over time to create personalized workout routines and nutrition plans that suit not just your body type but also your lifestyle.

Think about the sense of belonging these AI-powered apps can give you. As they get better at understanding you as an individual, they can provide advice tailored for you specifically - no generic one-size-fits-all programs here! It's like being part of a community where everyone gets their own custom-made plan. Whether it's suggesting new exercises to target specific muscles based on your progress or recommending meals that cater to both your nutritional needs and taste buds, these apps aim to make every aspect of health management truly personal.

And it doesn't stop there! The beauty of AI is its ability to continuously adapt as per the data fed into it. So instead of sticking with the same routine week after week, these intelligent applications evolve with you as they recognize changes in your performance, preference, or even mood!

Now that we've got a handle on how AI technology integrates into our pursuit for fitness, let's delve deeper into shaping this experience around our unique selves by identifying our individual needs and preferences. After all, tailoring is key when aiming for sustainable lifestyle changes rather than quick fixes.

Identifying Your Individual Needs and Preferences

Isn't it fascinating how your body, with its unique needs and preferences, can be the compass guiding you towards optimal well-being? Imagine having a tailored workout routine and nutrition plan that respects your individuality. AI-based health and fitness apps offer this exact experience. By understanding your specific requirements, they help you carve out a path to fitness that is uniquely yours.

Now, let's dive deeper into the process of identifying your individual needs and preferences:

Firstly, these smart apps inquire about your current lifestyle, including activity level and eating habits.

They then ask for crucial information like age, weight, height, and gender, which are fundamental to creating a personalized program.

Your specific goals are taken into account - whether you want to lose weight, gain muscle mass, or maintain optimal health.

Information related to any health conditions or physical limitations are also considered as they significantly affect the type of exercises suggested.

Lastly, they incorporate feedback loops where users can report back their progress or any challenges faced during workouts or diet plans.

By doing so, AI-based fitness apps ensure every aspect of your life is considered while designing an effective plan just for you. You're more than just numbers on a scale; you're an individual with distinct needs. And isn't it time we stopped following generic advice aimed at everyone else?

So now that we've figured out how important it is to understand our unique bodies in order to craft the perfect regime using these innovative tools! But remember, it doesn't end here; customization is key when striving towards our fitness aspirations.

Let's delve further into how we can tailor our exercise regimes using artificial intelligence in the next section...

Customizing Your Exercise Regime

So, ready to craft a fitness regimen that's uniquely tailored to your needs? Well, you're in luck. AI-based health and fitness apps are here to save the day, making it simpler than ever before.

These smart tools take into account your personal goals, preferences, physical limitations, and even time constraints to devise an exercise routine just for you. Whether you're a morning person who loves cardio or a night owl who prefers weightlifting, these apps have got you covered.

The beauty of these AI apps is their ability to adapt as your body does. Say goodbye to plateauing results; these programs evolve with your progress. They adjust the intensity of your workouts based on how well you are performing and achieving your set targets - all in real time!

So if you've been working hard and gaining strength faster than expected, the app will automatically make your workouts more challenging. It's like having a personal trainer right in your pocket!

But don't forget that exercise is only one part of the equation when it comes to leading a healthier lifestyle. To truly unlock optimal health benefits from your personalized workout regime, combining it with appropriate nutritional intake is key - And yes, AI-powered health and fitness apps can help here too!

Hang tight as we dive into how these revolutionary tools can assist in tailoring your diet for optimal results next.

Tailoring Your Diet for Optimal Results

Just as exercise regimes need to be custom-tailored for maximum effectiveness, the same applies to your diet - it's not just about what you eat, but when and how much.

You see, everyone's body is unique and responds differently to various types of food. Hence, a one-size-fits-all approach doesn't work when it comes to nutrition. AI-based health and fitness apps provide personalized diet plans based on scientific algorithms that consider your age, weight, lifestyle habits, medical history, and nutritional needs.

Here are some ways these apps can help you tailor your diet for optimal results:

- **Understand Your Nutritional Needs**: By determining the right balance of macronutrients (carbohydrates, protein, fats) and micronutrients (vitamins and minerals), the app ensures that every meal contributes towards fulfilling your daily nutrition requirements.

- **Manage Portion Size**: The app calculates appropriate portion sizes for each meal ensuring you're eating enough to fuel your workouts but not so much that it hampers weight loss or other fitness goals.

- **Timing Is Everything**: It helps you understand when the best times are to consume certain foods in order to maximize nutrient absorption.

Notice how all this attention to detail creates a sense of unity? We're all in this together; we're all trying our best to live healthier lives. These AI-based apps are like having a personal nutritionist at our fingertips who understands us better than anyone else. They guide us through complex nutritional landscapes with ease and precision so we can focus on staying active and feeling good without worrying about the minutiae.

So let's embrace this technology-driven era by using tools that make our journey towards health easier! Remember though: even with perfect diets tailored just for you, progress might be slow sometimes. But don't worry - steady wins the race! As long as we keep monitoring our progress closely with these apps' tracking features while adapting our routines accordingly for continuous improvement – reaching those wellness goals will not remain a distant dream anymore but an achievable reality on its way!

Monitoring Progress and Adapting for Improvement

Tracking your progress doesn't have to be a chore, especially when you've got the right tools at your fingertips. Imagine having a personal trainer and nutritionist in your pocket, available 24/7 - that's what AI-based health and fitness apps can offer.

These intuitive apps not only provide personalized workout routines and diet plans but also track your progress in real-time. They monitor everything from the number of steps you take to the calories you consume, providing an easy way for you to see how far you've come.

Take advantage of these technological marvels by consistently updating your data – yes, even those cheat days need to go in there! By doing so, these intelligent programs can adapt and adjust based on your performance and dietary habits.

Did a muscle group respond well to a particular exercise? The app will make note of it for future routines. Did a certain meal leave you feeling bloated or low-energy? The app can help identify potential food sensitivities or suggest healthier alternatives.

Remember that every journey is unique, just like each one of us. There may be bumps along the road—times when progress seems slow or almost non-existent—but don't let that derail you from your goals. Your AI companion is there to motivate and guide through all ups and downs.

It's about embracing this innovative technology as part of our wellness journey - because we're all in this together striving for better health, improved fitness levels, and ultimately achieving our best selves.

Frequently Asked Questions

What are the privacy concerns when using AI-based health and fitness apps?

You might worry about your personal data when using AI-based fitness apps. They often require access to sensitive health information, which raises concerns over privacy breaches and how this data might be used or shared.

How do these apps ensure the accuracy of the information provided?

You'll be over the moon to know these apps utilize advanced algorithms and data analytics, ensuring you're not just part of the crowd, but receiving accurate, personalized fitness advice tailored to your unique goals.

Are these apps recommended for people with specific health conditions like heart disease or diabetes?

Absolutely! These apps can be tailored to your unique health needs, including heart disease or diabetes. They're your digital companions, guiding you in leading a healthy lifestyle while keeping tabs on your specific conditions.

Can these apps replace the need for a personal trainer or dietitian?

While these apps can certainly guide you, they aren't a total replacement for a personal trainer or dietitian. They're tools to complement your wellness journey, but human expertise still holds immense value. You're not alone!

What's the cost of using these AI-based health and fitness apps?

Imagine yourself enjoying a personal trainer experience, but at a fraction of the cost. That's what AI-based fitness apps offer! They typically range from free to $15 per month, making them an affordable wellness companion.

Conclusion

In the grand symphony of your well-being, AI-based health and fitness apps play a crucial role. They're not just handy tools; they're personal trainers and nutritionists tucked in your pocket, helping you sculpt the masterpiece that is your body.

Don't let this high-tech ally gather dust. Embrace it, dance with it on your journey to peak fitness. With tailored workouts and diet plans at your fingertips, you hold the power to paint a healthier future.

You've got this!

AI-Driven Wearable Devices for Tracking Health Metrics and Encouraging Healthy Habits

You're living in an era where technology is rapidly evolving, and it's reshaping how you manage your health and wellness.

What if you could keep a close eye on your daily physical activities, monitor your heartbeat, track your sleep pattern or even receive personalized fitness advice - all from a tiny device strapped around your wrist? Welcome to the world of AI-driven wearable devices!

These smart gadgets are not just fashionable accessories; they're powerful tools designed to help you understand yourself better and make informed decisions about your health.

Now imagine being part of a global community that shares this same passion for health and well-being.

A community that harnesses the power of cutting-edge technology to inspire healthy habits, encourage personal growth, and foster deep connections with others who are on the same journey.

As you delve into this section, you'll discover how these ingenious devices work, their amazing features and benefits, insights they provide for making health decisions, and what exciting developments await in the future of personal health gadgets.

You're not alone - join us as we explore this fascinating intersection of technology and wellness!

Key Takeaways

- AI-driven wearable devices provide comprehensive insights into our overall well-being, allowing us to monitor physical activities, track sleep patterns, and receive personalized fitness advice.
- These devices empower individuals to understand themselves better and make informed decisions about their health, setting realistic fitness goals and tracking progress in real-time.
- AI-driven wearable devices foster healthy habits through continuous engagement and positive reinforcement, encouraging users to move, hydrate, and maintain an active lifestyle.
- The future of personal health gadgets holds the potential for even more advanced tracking of health metrics, such as blood pressure and stress levels, revolutionizing preventative healthcare.

The Rise of Personal Health Monitoring

You're now living in an era where personal health monitoring is skyrocketing, enabling you to keep a mindful eye on your health stats and foster wellness habits like never before. This surge isn't just about keeping tabs on your heart rate or the number of steps you've walked during the day; it's about having a deeper understanding of your overall well-being.

Features and Benefits of Smartwatches

Imagine having a personal assistant right on your wrist – smartwatches aren't just about telling time anymore. They're packed with features that can truly transform your day-to-day life! They've evolved into a platform providing an array of information. From tracking your steps to monitoring your heart rate, you'll be part of an innovative community where technology meets health and fitness. Feel the sense of belonging as you sync up with friends for friendly competitions or share your latest workout routine.

You'd be amazed at how a tiny device strapped to your wrist can offer such immense benefits. It's like wearing a mini-computer that keeps you updated on various aspects of your health, nudges you when it's time to get moving or hydrate, and even helps in sleep tracking and stress management. Whether it's pushing you towards achieving daily fitness goals or helping maintain mental wellness through mindfulness exercises – these devices are all about promoting healthier habits in a fun and interactive way. A smartwatch is more than just another tech gadget; it's a lifestyle choice that helps foster camaraderie among its users.

As we delve deeper into the world of AI-driven wearable devices, it becomes clear how influential this technology can be in facilitating better health choices. These devices provide real-time data enabling us to understand our bodies better – from sleeping patterns to caloric intake. This empowers us to make informed decisions about our health routines without feeling overwhelmed by complicated medical jargon or charts.

Let's now explore further how this intelligent technology enables us to make these savvy health decisions effortlessly.

Making Informed Health Decisions

With a smartwatch on your wrist, it's like having a personal coach that provides real-time insights into your body's functioning, making it easier for you to make informed decisions about your fitness and wellness routines. You can track various health metrics such as heart rate, sleep quality, step count, calories burned, and even stress levels.

All this information at your disposal makes it possible to understand how changes in lifestyle habits affect overall well-being. This way, you're not just blindly following diet plans or workout regimes; instead, you're making choices based on personalized data.

It helps you set realistic fitness goals based on your daily activity level.

By tracking sleep patterns and quality, it prompts better sleeping habits.

The device alerts if there's an unusual spike in heart rate or drop in blood oxygen levels - helping to detect potential health issues early.

Regular reminders to move or hydrate encourage healthier habits throughout the day.

No one knows your body better than yourself. But sometimes we need assistance interpreting what our bodies are trying to tell us – that's where AI-driven wearable devices come into play. They provide tangible evidence of what works for us and what doesn't when it comes to maintaining our health and improving fitness levels.

As these devices become more advanced over time with greater accuracy and functionalities - they will be invaluable tools in encouraging healthier lifestyles.

Entering the era of personal health gadgets is akin to embarking upon a journey towards self-awareness and proactive health management. Now let's look forward to how technology may further revolutionize the world of personal health care in the future sections.

The Future of Personal Health Gadgets

You're on the cusp of a revolution, much like when man first stepped on the moon, as we delve deeper into what the future holds for personal health gadgets. These AI-driven wearable devices are becoming your personal health coaches, tracking everything from heart rate and sleep patterns to blood pressure and stress levels.

They're more than just fitness trackers; they're giving you a holistic view of your health in real-time. And with this information at your fingertips, you can take control of your wellbeing like never before.

Imagine waking up each day to personalised insights about your body's needs that day. Your smartwatch could recommend a brisk walk if it detects high stress levels or suggest you hydrate more after identifying low fluid intake. It's about fostering healthy habits through continuous engagement and positive reinforcement—making good health feel less like a chore and more like an accomplishment. Because let's face it—who wouldn't want to be part of a community that prioritizes their well-being?

As we move forward, these wearables will become even smarter and more tailored to individual needs. They'll be able to predict potential health issues even before symptoms arise based on data trends collected over time—an impressive feat that could change the landscape of preventative healthcare.

The future is here—and it looks incredibly healthy! So strap on that smartwatch, lace up those running shoes, and join us in this exciting journey towards better health care management with the power of AI technology right at our wrists!

Frequently Asked Questions

What are the potential privacy concerns with using AI-driven wearable devices for health tracking?

You might worry about your personal health details being exposed or misused. These smart devices hold intimate information, which if mishandled, could potentially lead to identity theft or reveal sensitive health-related issues.

Are there any known health risks associated with the long-term use of these devices?

Sure, while these wearables are generally safe, long-term use can potentially cause skin irritation or allergic reactions. It's also vital to manage your screen time to avoid digital eye strain. Always prioritize your wellbeing!

How accurate are the health metrics provided by these AI-driven wearable devices in comparison to traditional medical equipment?

Like comparing apples to oranges, AI-driven wearables may not match traditional medical equipment's precision. Still, they provide fairly accurate data that can help you stay tuned with your health and feel connected.

Can these devices be used by individuals with specific health conditions, such as heart disease or diabetes?

Absolutely! You with heart disease or diabetes can benefit greatly. These devices help monitor your health, alerting you to changes that might need a doctor's attention. You're not alone—let these wearables aid in your journey.

What are some of the limitations or drawbacks of relying on wearable technology for health monitoring?

While wearables can be handy, they're not foolproof. They may miss subtle health changes and aren't a replacement for professional medical advice. Plus, privacy issues arise as personal health data gets shared with companies.

Conclusion

You've taken a thrilling journey into the world of AI-powered wearables, haven't you? It's like embarking on a spaceship to unexplored territory in the universe of health and fitness. These savvy gadgets are your co-pilots, guiding you towards better health choices and pushing you to embrace healthier habits.

So strap on that smartwatch or fitness band, folks! The future of personal health is here - it's as bright as a supernova and just as exciting. Let's explore this galaxy together!

AI's Role in Early Disease Detection and Telemedicine Services

Welcome! You're now stepping into the future of healthcare, a world where artificial intelligence (AI) is revolutionizing early disease detection and telemedicine services.

Imagine this: you receive healthcare consultation from your couch's comfort and get diagnosed for potential health issues even before they begin to manifest symptoms. Yes, that's how transformative AI has become in shaping our healthcare landscape.

Now, you might be wondering how all this works? Well, buckle up! We're about to dive deep into the world of predictive analysis and machine learning that are making these groundbreaking changes possible.

With AI's help, doctors can offer virtual consultations more effectively while also monitoring patients remotely with unprecedented efficiency.

Together we'll explore the power of AI in advancing accessibility and efficacy in healthcare like never before. It's not just about being part of a new era; it's about being part of a community that embraces progress for everyone's wellbeing.

Key Takeaways

- AI in healthcare is revolutionizing early disease detection and telemedicine services.
- Predictive analysis and machine learning are making groundbreaking changes possible.
- AI empowers healthcare providers to identify diseases earlier and offer personalized treatment plans based on individual risk factors.
- Telemedicine services provide convenience, accessibility, and inclusivity by allowing healthcare consultations from the comfort of one's own home and enabling remote patient monitoring.

The Power of Predictive Analysis in Healthcare

There's no denying that the power of predictive analysis in healthcare, bolstered by AI, can dramatically improve early disease detection and revolutionize telemedicine services.

Visualize a world where diseases are detected even before symptoms occur - sounds like science fiction, right? But thanks to AI and predictive analytics, this is becoming a reality.

Predictive models use historical patient data to anticipate potential health risks, giving doctors an edge in diagnosing illnesses earlier than ever before.

Imagine being part of an innovative community that utilizes advanced tools for better health outcomes. The beauty of this technology lies not only in its capability to predict future health conditions but also in its capacity to personalize treatment plans based on individual risk factors. This means you'll receive care specially tailored for you!

Wouldn't it be comforting knowing that your medical team uses cutting-edge tech to ensure your wellbeing?

The transformative potential of predictive analytics doesn't stop there. It offers far-reaching benefits that extend into the realm of telemedicine services. By leveraging these powerful tools, healthcare providers can offer more proactive remote care with precision and efficiency never seen before.

And as we delve deeper into how machine learning is revolutionizing patient diagnosis, you'll see just how integral AI has become in transforming our healthcare landscape for the better.

Revolutionizing Patient Diagnosis with Machine Learning

Who'd have thought that machine learning, a concept as nerdy as pocket protectors and slide rules, could turn the world of patient diagnosis on its head?

But here we are in an era where artificial intelligence empowers healthcare providers to identify diseases earlier than ever before. Imagine not having to wait for symptoms to show up or those prolonged, anxious doctor visits. Instead, with machine learning algorithms sifting through huge volumes of data - from your medical history to population health statistics - you can receive accurate diagnoses and treatment plans swiftly.

Picture this: You belong to a community where every person is given the chance for early intervention because of AI's predictive prowess. Machine learning doesn't just make educated guesses; it learns from patterns in vast amounts of data and provides concrete evidence-based results.

It's like having a detective who never sleeps, tirelessly working behind the scenes, studying all aspects of your health data. By spotting trends and anomalies that might be missed by human eyes, machine learning offers you personalized care while promoting better overall community health.

What's more exciting? The revolution doesn't stop there! This cutting-edge technology works hand-in-hand with telemedicine services offering remote patient monitoring capabilities. You don't need to leave home or take time off work for routine check-ups; instead, these virtual consultations provide real-time updates about your health status directly to your healthcare provider.

So buckle up! With this dynamic duo of machine learning and telemedicine at our disposal, we're on the brink of an exciting new chapter in healthcare: the emergence of virtual healthcare consultations.

The Emergence of Virtual Healthcare Consultations

You're now stepping into an era where virtual healthcare consultations aren't just a concept but an emerging reality, transforming the way we perceive and experience medical care. Imagine the convenience of chatting with your doctor from your cozy living room, having prescriptions refilled without ever leaving home, or receiving health advice at any hour of the day or night.

Welcome to this new age of telemedicine services powered by AI - it's like being part of a futuristic sci-fi novel but it's happening right here in our present. And it's not just about comfort and convenience; it's also about accessibility and inclusivity.

For those living in remote areas or facing mobility challenges, this digital revolution provides a lifeline, ensuring that quality healthcare isn't a privilege but a right for all. Isn't that something you'd like to be part of? A movement towards democratizing healthcare through technology and artificial intelligence! It's exciting how AI has made healthcare more inclusive and accessible; truly, we're witnessing radical changes in how doctors diagnose, treat patients remotely, and provide personalized care.

Yet the marvels don't stop there. This blend of telemedicine services with AI is paving the way for another groundbreaking innovation: remote patient monitoring. Get ready as we delve deep into this next frontier where continuous health tracking becomes possible regardless of geographical boundaries or time limitations.

The future looks promising indeed with these advancements that make us feel more connected to our health than ever before!

Remote Patient Monitoring and AI

Brace yourself for boundless benefits brought by breakthroughs in remote patient monitoring. Thanks to artificial intelligence (AI), healthcare providers can now monitor your health conditions remotely, without the need for you to step foot into a hospital or medical facility.

This technology not only offers convenience but also real-time updates about your health status, ensuring that any anomalies are detected early and addressed promptly.

As part of this exciting advancement, AI takes on multiple roles:

- **Predictive Analytics**: AI uses sophisticated algorithms to analyze your health data and flag potential health risks before they become serious.
- **Real-Time Monitoring**: Wearable devices empowered with AI can track vital signs like heart rate, blood pressure, and oxygen saturation levels continuously. This constant surveillance allows quick response to any sudden changes in your condition.
- **Personalized Care Plans**: Based on the collected data and its analysis, AI can help formulate personalized care plans that cater specifically to your unique needs.

What's powerful about these capabilities is their inherent inclusivity. Everyone stands to gain - from those living in remote areas with limited access to healthcare facilities, people struggling with chronic conditions who require constant monitoring, or just folks looking for preventive care methods.

The beauty of it lies within its ability to empower you as an active participant in managing your own health instead of being a passive recipient of care. Imagine having control over your wellness at the tip of your fingers!

This revolution brought about by remote patient monitoring and AI is transforming how we perceive healthcare delivery models. It's not just about treating illnesses anymore; it's about proactively managing one's well-being.

Just think: isn't it wonderful how technology is advancing accessibility and efficiency in healthcare?

Let us delve deeper into how this shift could reshape our lives even further in the next section.

Advancing Accessibility and Efficiency in Healthcare

It's like having a 24/7 personal healthcare assistant right in your pocket, making medical care easily accessible and efficient regardless of location or time.

Imagine not having to wait weeks for an appointment, or sit in a waiting room full of sniffles and sneezes. Instead, with the power of artificial intelligence (AI) and telemedicine, you can connect with healthcare professionals from the comfort of your own home. Whether it's 2 AM or 2 PM, there's always someone ready to listen to your health concerns.

Imagine being part of a community where everyone is cared for equally – where the struggle to access quality healthcare doesn't exist because AI has leveled the playing field.

With smart wearable devices tracking vital signs and AI algorithms detecting early warning symptoms, you're no longer just another patient in a crowded hospital; you're part of an interconnected network that values proactive health management. These advancements are not just about convenience - they represent a revolutionary shift towards personalized care tailored specifically for you.

As we move forward into this new era of digital health services, let's remember that technology isn't replacing human touch but enhancing it. The integration of AI into telemedicine services brings us one step closer to achieving universal healthcare coverage while also fostering a sense of belonging among patients globally.

It's reshaping how we view our health - by putting control back into our hands and creating a sense of community where every individual matters.

This is more than just medical advancement; it's about building bridges within humanity through compassionate care accessible anywhere at any time.

Frequently Asked Questions

How does patient privacy and data security get maintained in AI-enabled healthcare services?

Just by chance, you're curious about patient privacy in AI healthcare? Well, they use top-notch encryption and strict access controls. You're part of a world where your health data stays confidential, even with AI involved.

Can AI in healthcare completely replace the need for human medical professionals?

While AI can enhance healthcare, it won't completely replace human medical professionals. You'll still need the personal touch, empathy, and nuanced decision-making that only doctors can provide. Remember, machines assist; they don't replace.

How does AI interact and collaborate with other technologies like IoT in healthcare?

You're part of a tech-savvy community leveraging AI and IoT in healthcare. They collaborate seamlessly, with IoT devices gathering patient data and AI analyzing it for early disease detection or personalized telemedicine services.

What are the potential risks or limitations of AI in early disease detection and telemedicine services?

Imagine stepping into a world where technology rules. While AI offers promising advancements in healthcare, it's not without risks. It may misinterpret data, leading to wrong diagnoses and privacy concerns can arise with telemedicine services.

Are AI-enabled healthcare services affordable for all types of patients?

Absolutely, AI-enabled healthcare isn't just for the wealthy. It's democratizing healthcare, making it accessible and affordable to everyone. No matter who you are or where you're from, these services can be within your reach.

Conclusion

Imagine, you're on a routine check-up, and your doctor already knows the potential health risks you might face in the future. AI's predictive analysis is making this possible.

But that's not all, with machine learning revolutionizing diagnosis, they can detect diseases earlier than ever.

Now picture this - virtual consultations and remote monitoring systems meaning you never have to step foot in a hospital again unless absolutely necessary. That's the power of AI; increasing accessibility while boosting efficiency in healthcare.

Chapter 7: AI and Education

AI-Powered Language Learning Platforms for Mastering New Languages

Imagine you're in the heart of Tokyo, navigating through bustling streets, vibrant neon lights buzzing overhead. You're trying to ask a local for directions, but there's just one problem - you don't speak Japanese.

But wait! With AI-powered language learning platforms at your fingertips, mastering a new language is easier than ever before.

Ever felt that longing for belonging while traveling or moving to a new country? The desire to fit in and communicate effectively with locals can be quite strong. Thanks to advancements in technology, particularly Artificial Intelligence (AI), you no longer have to feel like an outsider.

These innovative platforms are personalizing lessons, offering real-time feedback and tracking progress effortlessly. So get ready to explore how these tools are changing the game of language learning and enabling people globally to become multilingual with ease.

Key Takeaways
- AI-powered language learning platforms revolutionize the language learning experience by offering personalized lessons, real-time feedback, and progress tracking.
- These platforms understand individual learning styles and provide tailored content, creating immersive learning environments that mimic real-life conversations.
- AI-powered language learning platforms simplify the process of acquiring new languages, providing access to different cultures, thoughts, ideas, and perspectives.
- When choosing an AI-powered platform, it is important to consider factors such as motivation, learning style, time availability, and accessibility.

Understanding the Role of Technology in Education

You've got to realize that technology's role in education isn't just about flashy gadgets and apps, it's about how these tools can truly revolutionize your learning experience and take language mastery to a whole new level.

It's not about replacing traditional teaching methods, but rather enhancing them with advanced digital resources. You see, when you start incorporating AI-powered platforms into your language-learning journey, you're not only adopting a modern approach—you're also becoming part of an innovative community that values progressive learning techniques.

Imagine being part of a platform where the computer understands your individual learning style, adjusts the pace accordingly, and offers personalized content based on your preferences and needs. This is more than just convenience—it's a revolutionary step towards adaptive education.

With AI technologies like natural language processing (NLP) and machine learning algorithms at work behind the scenes, you'll find yourself immersed in an interactive environment that mimics real-life conversations. You're no longer limited by geographical boundaries or fixed classroom schedules; instead, you're connected to a global community of learners who share your aspirations.

This fascinating shift towards tech-enhanced education brings us one step closer to making tailored learning experiences accessible for everyone. Imagine having lessons tailored specifically to your strengths and weaknesses—doesn't that sound incredibly empowering?

The beauty of this trend is that it personalizes the entire process of mastering new languages—making education feel less like a chore and more like an intriguing adventure designed exclusively for you! As we move forward discussing AI-powered language platforms' potential advantages, let's delve deeper into our next topic: unlocking the benefits of personalized lessons.

Benefits of Personalized Lessons

In the realm of personalized lessons, your progress isn't maintained by a steam engine train; it's more like a sleek bullet train that adjusts its speed and direction according to your own unique learning curve.

With AI-powered language learning platforms, you're not just another passenger on the journey to language mastery. These intelligent systems understand that everyone learns differently and tailors lessons to meet your specific needs. Just imagine having a private coach who knows exactly where you excel and where you need improvement - all while operating at an optimal pace tailored for you.

Here are four key benefits of personalized lessons in AI-powered language learning:

1. **Custom-tailored Content:** The platform understands your strengths, weaknesses, and interests which translates into relevant content designed specifically for you.

2. **Adaptive Learning Pace:** Your learning speed is respected here; sometimes it's fast-paced, other times slower but always matched with your comprehension level.

3. **Real-Time Adjustment:** The system adapts instantaneously based on how well or poorly you're progressing within a particular lesson.

4. **Enhanced Engagement:** Lessons incorporate topics that hold your interest leading to higher engagement levels and improved retention rates.

You see, personalized lessons are all about making sure that no learner feels left out or overwhelmed in their quest for language proficiency. They offer an ideal balance between challenge and ability which keeps motivation high throughout the journey without causing unnecessary frustration or burnout.

This way, every single moment spent studying languages becomes meaningful, rewarding, and enjoyable - not a dreadful chore to tick off from your daily schedule! As we dive deeper into this captivating world of AI-enabled education tools, let's shift our focus onto real-time feedback mechanisms because they play an integral role in ensuring consistent progress towards mastering new languages.

Real-Time Feedback and Progress Tracking

Imagine having a personal guide who not only navigates your journey through the intricacies of linguistic nuances but also keeps track of how far you've come and what lies ahead. That's exactly what AI-powered language learning platforms offer, providing real-time feedback and progress tracking capabilities.

As you master new words, phrases, and grammatical rules, these platforms keep tabs on your growth, highlighting your strengths while identifying areas where you may need more practice. It's like having a personalized coach who celebrates your wins with you and gently nudges you towards overcoming challenges.

Isn't it reassuring to know exactly where you stand on the road to mastering a new language? With real-time feedback from AI systems, there's no room for guesswork or uncertainty about your proficiency level. You get immediate corrections and advice during practice sessions, helping you avoid ingraining incorrect habits.

The interactive nature of these platforms fosters an engaging learning environment that makes language acquisition feel less like an academic chore and more like an exciting adventure that you're part of.

The beauty of this intelligent technology isn't just in its ability to monitor your progress; it paves the way for a richer connection with people around the world as well. After all, nothing conjures up a sense of belonging quite like being able to communicate fluently in another person's native tongue! This seamless integration into diverse cultures is one aspect that truly sets AI-enhanced language learning apart.

Now imagine extending this personal achievement further: by exploring how multilingualism can have a profound global impact - that's our next fascinating topic!

Exploring the Global Impact of Multilingualism

Isn't it astounding that over half of the world's population is bilingual or multilingual? That's right, more than 50% of people worldwide can speak at least two languages.

This remarkable fact underscores the immense power and influence of multilingualism in fostering global connections and understanding. Understanding multiple languages gives you access to a variety of cultures, thoughts, ideas, and perspectives that you wouldn't otherwise be privy to. It broadens your horizon in ways unimaginable.

Now consider this: what if everyone could easily learn new languages? What if barriers like time, resources, or difficulty level didn't exist?

AI-powered language learning platforms are making this dream a reality by simplifying the process of acquiring new languages. They're not just teaching grammar rules and vocabulary lists; they're providing immersive experiences that make learning feel less like studying and more like exploring a different culture. You'll feel closer to other societies without even leaving your home – an experience akin to becoming part of a worldwide family.

The global impact of such inclusive tools can't be overstated. From enhancing cross-cultural communication to breaking down societal barriers – these platforms have enormous potential benefits for our interconnected world.

As you contemplate mastering another language, think about the ripple effect it could create; think about how it could change your life and maybe even the world around you! Imagine drifting effortlessly from one conversation to another in various languages, being able to understand different viewpoints better because now you share a common linguistic bond with others. The thrill is worth every bit!

Now let's help guide you towards choosing the tool that will best help unlock these possibilities for you.

Choosing the Right Tool for Your Needs

As you embark on this linguistic journey, it's crucial to select a tool that aligns perfectly with your specific requirements and learning style. You're not just looking for any old language app; you want something that truly understands and adapts to your unique needs.

The world of AI-powered language learning platforms is vast, diverse, and always evolving. It's like an exciting marketplace where each platform has its own distinctive features designed to enhance your language mastery process. Some offer immersive experiences with native speakers, others use machine learning algorithms for personalized lesson plans or gamified exercises.

Taking the time to explore these options can be both thrilling and somewhat overwhelming as you try to find your place in this global community of language learners - but don't worry! Remember that everyone here is also pursuing their own path towards multilingualism, just like you are right now. We all share a common passion for exploring new cultures through their languages, creating a sense of unity and belonging despite our different starting points or destinations.

Choosing the right AI-powered platform isn't about finding the one with the most features or the highest ratings; it's about finding the one that clicks with you on a personal level. Think about what motivates you to learn – do you thrive on interactive exercises? Or perhaps meticulously planned lessons? Consider how much time you have available each day – could micro-lessons fit better into your schedule? And don't forget about accessibility: should this tool be mobile-friendly so you can study on-the-go?

These are all essential questions to ask yourself when choosing among various platforms. Feel confident in making this decision because ultimately it's all part of shaping your unique journey towards mastering new languages.

Frequently Asked Questions

What are the limitations of using AI for language learning?

You might think AI is the ultimate language guru, but it's not quite there yet. AI can't replicate human interaction or cultural nuances perfectly. It also struggles to provide feedback like a real teacher would.

How is the privacy of learners ensured on these AI-powered platforms?

Your privacy is a priority! These platforms use advanced encryption and strict data protocols to keep your information safe. They're like private tutors, only interested in your language progress and not in invading your space.

Are there any age restrictions or recommended age groups for using these platforms?

Did you know 74% of language learners start young? There's no age limit on curiosity! These platforms are suitable for all, but kids under 13 need parental consent. You're never too old or too young to belong and learn.

Can AI-powered language learning replace traditional classroom learning completely?

While AI-powered learning can enhance your language skills, it doesn't entirely replace traditional classroom learning. You'll miss out on real-time interactions and cultural nuances that only a classroom environment can offer. Balance is key!

How much time on average does it take to master a new language using these platforms?

Throwing caution to the wind, you jump in. The time it takes depends on your dedication and frequency of use. However, many find that with daily use, fluency can be reached within 4-6 months.

Conclusion

Just like the Babel fish in 'Hitchhiker's Guide to the Galaxy,' AI-powered platforms are becoming your ultimate language translators, enabling you to conquer linguistic barriers.

They're not just teaching you languages, they're opening doors to new worlds.

So take the leap! Choose the right tool and embark on this exciting journey of learning a new language.

Remember, every word you master is a step towards embracing diversity and fostering global connections.

Let technology be your guide on this enlightening voyage.

Adaptive Learning Systems and AI Tutors for Personalized Education Paths

Have you ever wondered how education can be tailored to meet your unique learning style? A one-size-fits-all approach isn't always the most effective way to learn. With advancements in technology, education is evolving beyond traditional methods and approaching a more individualized style of instruction. Imagine having a personalized AI tutor that adapts its teaching methods based on your strengths and weaknesses, paving the way towards an enriched learning experience.

In today's digital age, adaptive learning systems are transforming the education landscape. These revolutionary tools utilize artificial intelligence to provide personalized educational paths, enhancing student engagement and fostering academic growth. You're no longer a face in the crowd but rather an active participant in your own educational journey. This shift towards digitalized education isn't just about keeping up with technology; it's about creating a sense of belonging where every learner feels seen, understood, and valued.

Key Takeaways

- Education is shifting towards a more individualized style of instruction, with personalized AI tutors and adaptive learning systems.
- Personalized education promotes better understanding, retention of knowledge, and emotional development.
- AI tutors enhance teachers' capabilities and make personalized learning more feasible by providing immediate feedback, answering questions, and suggesting additional resources.
- Adaptive learning systems play a pivotal role in education by tailoring instruction to individual needs, tastes, and preferences, making each lesson feel tailor-made for students and increasing their engagement.

The Evolution of Modern Teaching Methods

You've witnessed how modern teaching methods have evolved, haven't you? They've seamlessly transitioned from traditional chalk-and-talk to adaptive learning systems and AI tutors, personalizing education paths like never before. This evolution hasn't been a mere change; it's an upgrade that has revolutionized the way we learn.

It's like opening a door into a world where each individual's unique learning style is respected and catered for. Can you feel how this connects us all to the heart of education? Envision yourself in this new educational setting: your pace, your style, no more one-size-fits-all approach. You're not just another face in the crowd; you're being understood on a deeper level by these advanced learning tools which adapt their teaching strategies based on your performance and needs.

Isn't it empowering to know that these intelligent systems are designed with you in mind, striving tirelessly to make every bit of knowledge digestible and accessible for you? It gives you a sense of belonging, doesn't it?

This isn't an abstract concept anymore; it's becoming our reality as AI tutors are increasingly used in classrooms worldwide. They aren't replacing teachers but rather enhancing their capabilities and making personalized learning more feasible than ever before.

No longer confined by traditional constraints, we now can explore limitless possibilities within our grasp thanks to these technological advancements. As we continue exploring the impact of adaptive learning systems on modern education methods, it further enhances our understanding of individualized instructional approaches.

Understanding Individualized Instructional Approaches

Grasping the complexity of individualized instructional approaches, it's essential to understand that each student possesses distinct educational needs and learning styles. This means that what works for one learner might not be effective for another.

It's about recognizing and celebrating these differences, fostering an inclusive environment where everyone feels acknowledged and understood. Individualized instruction is no longer a luxury; it's a necessity in modern education.

The aim is to tailor teaching methods and content to meet each student's unique needs, thereby promoting better understanding and retention of knowledge.

Creating personalized paths in education isn't just about academic growth; it also nurtures emotional development by cultivating a sense of belonging among learners. When you see your learning style being recognized, when you feel that the system is genuinely working towards your success, you are more likely to engage with the process wholeheartedly.

You can overcome hurdles with confidence because you know that there's room for failure and growth within this system - there's no 'one-size-fits-all'. It creates an atmosphere where every voice matters, where every question contributes to collective wisdom.

As we venture deeper into this era of customized education, technology plays a pivotal role in facilitating these individualized experiences. Artificial Intelligence (AI) emerges as a powerful tool in transforming traditional classrooms into dynamic spaces tailored to accommodate diverse learning styles.

AI does not only revolutionize how teachers teach but also how students learn, paving the way for more meaningful encounters with knowledge. We're moving towards an exciting future where AI becomes our ally in crafting personalized educational journeys teeming with possibility and promise.

The Role of Artificial Intelligence in Education

Imagine this - your instruction tailored to your individual needs, tastes, and preferences, all thanks to the magic of artificial intelligence in education. No more sitting in a classroom struggling to keep up with concepts that are too advanced or getting bored with topics that are too easy for you.

AI tutors can take into account your unique learning style, pace, strengths, and weaknesses to create an education path designed just for you. With AI's adaptive learning systems, each lesson is transformed into an engaging experience where you're not just memorizing facts but truly understanding them. It's like having a personal tutor who knows exactly what you need to succeed and is always available when you need help.

These intelligent tutors can provide immediate feedback on your work, answer your questions instantly, and even suggest additional resources for further study if necessary. They also constantly adjust their teaching strategies based on your progress, ensuring that every minute spent studying is productive and meaningful.

The role of AI in education isn't limited just to enhancing personalized instruction; it has far-reaching implications for student engagement as well. By turning textbooks into interactive digital platforms or using virtual reality simulations for hands-on learning experiences, AI makes education more engaging than ever before.

This infusion of technology keeps students interested because they feel like they're part of something special – something bigger than themselves – rather than simply passive recipients of information.

So let's delve deeper into how such technological advancements are revolutionizing student engagement in the next section.

The Impact of Technology on Student Engagement

It's like diving into a vibrant, interactive book, where technology has breathed life into every page, captivating students and igniting their curiosity like never before. Your child isn't just observing from the sidelines anymore; they're in the thick of it all, interacting with lessons in a way that feels more akin to playing than learning.

Educational technology engages students on an unprecedented level. It fosters an environment where everyone feels involved and incorporated into the learning process, creating a sense of belonging that's so vital for effective education.

Imagine your child participating in virtual field trips around the world without leaving their classroom or engaging with complex mathematical concepts through an immersive game-based platform. These aren't far-fetched scenarios anymore but are becoming commonplace as educational institutions harness the power of technology to boost student engagement.

Adaptive learning systems provide personalized paths based on individual strengths and weaknesses, making each lesson feel tailor-made for them. This individualized approach not only captivates students' attention but also makes them active participants in their own education journey.

As we look forward to what lies ahead in this dynamic blend of technology and pedagogy, one thing is clear: digitalization is revolutionizing how our children learn. The physical boundaries of classrooms are being shattered as learning becomes a 24/7 endeavor available at students' fingertips; engagement is no longer confined within school hours or walls.

This shift towards digitized learning environments paves the way for us to explore uncharted territories about 'the future of digitalized education', where innovation will continue shaping our children's educational experiences.

The Future of Digitalized Education

You're stepping into a new era where the landscape of education is being transformed by digital technology, creating exciting possibilities for students and teachers alike.

Imagine a world where classrooms aren't limited by physical walls, but are expansive and accessible from any corner of the globe. This is not just about getting information at your fingertips; it's about creating personalized learning paths that adapt to your pace, strengths, and interests.

Isn't it thrilling to think about a future where every learner feels valued because learning materials and methods are uniquely tailored to suit their needs?

In this brave new world of digitalized education, adaptive learning systems play a pivotal role. Picture an AI tutor who knows you better than you know yourself - recognizing when you're struggling with a concept and providing extra support just when you need it most.

Imagine how much more engaging your lessons could be with interactive multimedia content that keeps you hooked on every word, every image or video clip! You would no longer feel left out because the system ensures that everyone's learning style is catered for.

As we look ahead at this promising horizon of digitalized education, unique opportunities for connection arise. Our classrooms become global communities bringing together diverse perspectives and experiences in an enriching melting pot of ideas.

The AI tutors don't merely dish out information; they foster collaborative interactions among learners from different backgrounds thus making us part of something bigger than ourselves. It's not only about acquiring knowledge anymore – it's also about belonging in our shared pursuit towards excellence in education.

Undoubtedly, embracing these advancements paves the path for an inclusive educational environment where everyone feels seen, heard and appreciated while achieving their full potential.

Frequently Asked Questions

What are the costs associated with implementing adaptive learning systems and AI tutors?

Ironically, nothing comes free. You'll face significant costs for software development, maintenance, training personnel and data management. Yet, these investments often result in a more inclusive learning environment where everyone feels part of the journey.

How can adaptive learning systems and AI tutors be integrated into traditional classroom settings?

You can blend adaptive learning systems and AI tutors into your classrooms by integrating them into lesson plans, using them for personalized homework assignments, or as supplementary tutoring for students who need extra assistance.

What are the potential challenges or limitations of using AI tutors for personalized education paths?

"Imagine running a race with hurdles, that's using AI tutors. They may lack human touch, struggle to understand complex emotions or cultural nuances, and pose data privacy issues. But remember, every hurdle is a stepping stone." 'Each challenge faced is an opportunity for growth and improvement, pushing us closer to the goal of quality, personalized, and accessible education for all.'

Are there any ethical concerns associated with the use of AI in education?

Absolutely, there are ethical concerns with AI in education. You might worry about privacy issues, data misuse, or algorithmic bias. It's essential to create a safe learning environment that respects everyone's rights and individuality.

How can adaptive learning systems and AI tutors address the diverse learning needs of students with special educational needs?

Adaptive learning systems and AI tutors can address diverse needs by customizing lessons for students with special educational needs. They adjust the pace, content, and delivery method to enhance understanding and engagement.

Conclusion

You've embarked on an exciting journey, haven't you? The realm of education is no longer a one-size-fits-all game. It's been reshaped, reborn into something more dynamic and personalised.

With AI tutors and adaptive learning systems, the way you learn is being fine-tuned to meet your unique needs.

But let's not sugarcoat it - we're just scratching the surface here. We're standing at the precipice of a new era in digitalized education. The future holds untold possibilities, so buckle up!

AI Tools for Enhancing Research and Studying Efficiency

You've always been on the lookout for ways to optimize your learning and research processes, haven't you? You've probably tried numerous strategies, from flashcards to mnemonic devices, all in an effort to boost your efficiency. But have you considered how artificial intelligence (AI) could revolutionize your approach? It's not just about robots and futuristic tech; AI tools can now play a significant role in enhancing research and studying efficiency.

Imagine a world where smart algorithms analyze vast amounts of data in seconds while automated systems adapt learning material based on individual needs. Picture yourself conducting academic research with advanced tech that saves time and increases accuracy. This isn't science fiction anymore; it's rapidly becoming our reality.

In this section, we'll explore how these amazing AI tools are reshaping education and research - making it more productive, personalized, and efficient. So welcome aboard! You're about to join a community of forward-thinking individuals who are harnessing the power of AI for educational advancement.

Key Takeaways

- AI tools can analyze vast amounts of data in seconds and adapt learning material based on individual needs.
- Smart algorithms simplify data analysis and foster collaboration, making research and studying processes more efficient.
- AI-powered online study groups can recognize individual strengths and weaknesses, enhancing personalized learning experiences.
- AI automation frees up researchers' time for critical thinking and problem-solving, empowering them to conduct more impactful research.

Understanding Machine Learning in Education

You're about to dive into the fascinating world of machine learning in education, where teaching and studying become more engaging and efficient than you've ever imagined.

Machine learning is transforming how we approach education, allowing for personalized learning experiences that cater to a student's individual strengths and weaknesses. It's not just about replacing textbooks with tablets or homework with apps; it's a paradigm shift towards an adaptive, responsive educational system designed to meet each learner where they are.

Imagine a classroom environment where teachers have access to real-time data on their students' performance and understanding. This isn't some far-fetched sci-fi scenario; it's happening right now thanks to machine learning algorithms!

These powerful tools can analyze countless data points from student interactions, identifying patterns and trends that might otherwise go unnoticed. This allows educators to tailor their instruction based on accurate insights into each student's progress, making the whole process more effective. You'd feel like you truly belong in this dynamic learning environment tailored just for you!

Let's put the spotlight now on smart algorithms used for data analysis within this context. These aren't your ordinary number-crunching mechanisms; these intelligent systems can sift through mountains of educational data - grades, attendance records, online activity - then distill it all down into actionable insights effortlessly.

Optimal decision-making becomes a breeze when armed with such vital information, leading not only to better academic outcomes but also fostering a sense of belonging among learners as they see their unique needs being addressed accurately. Just wait until we delve deeper into what these remarkable systems entail in our subsequent discussion!

Utilizing Smart Algorithms for Data Analysis

Harnessing the power of smart algorithms can revolutionize data analysis, offering profound insights that drive innovation and progress.

Imagine you're sitting in front of a massive pile of raw data - an intimidating chaos of numbers and facts. Without the right tools, making sense of this information could take weeks or even months, but with smart algorithms at your side, you can swiftly sift through these datasets to find patterns and trends that would be impossible to spot otherwise.

You're no longer just a researcher or student; you're a visionary explorer on the cutting edge of knowledge.

Smart algorithms are not just about crunching numbers—they are about creating community. They encourage collaboration by bringing people together around shared goals and communal challenges.

Whether you're part of an academic team seeking to answer complex questions or a study group aiming for top grades, these powerful tools amplify your efforts by helping everyone get on the same page quickly and effectively. Remember that feeling when everything clicks into place? That's what it feels like to work with smart algorithms - it's as if you've suddenly found the key to unlock all those challenging puzzles.

But there's more! Beyond simplifying data analysis, these AI-powered tools open doors to new ways we learn and grow academically. They streamline processes making them more efficient while reducing mistakes often associated with manual workloads.

This way, they leave us extra time for meaningful engagement in our studies instead of getting lost in tedious tasks. Picture yourself spending less time wrestling with spreadsheets and more time diving deep into subjects that truly captivate your interest – sounds amazing, right?

And as we turn our gaze forward towards 'the role of automated systems in learning', prepare to discover how much further these innovative technologies can take us.

The Role of Automated Systems in Learning

Automated systems are transforming the landscape of education, and it's astounding to know that nearly 50% of higher education institutions now utilize some form of automation in learning, according to a report by eLearning Industry. These systems not only enhance how you study but also significantly increase your efficiency.

You've probably been part of a class where you struggled with the pace or needed more time on a certain topic. Automated systems curate personalized learning paths based on your individual needs, ensuring no one is left behind or overlooked.

Remember those late-night cram sessions before exams? With automated tools like flashcards, adaptive quizzes, and smart reminders, those might become relics of the past. The beauty lies in these tools' ability to adapt as per your learning habits and patterns; they learn from you just as much as you learn from them. Imagine having an AI-powered tutor available round-the-clock at your service, ready to help whenever you need, without any judgment or impatience – feels incredibly supportive, doesn't it?

Beyond automating repetitive tasks and enhancing personalized learning experiences in schools and universities alike, these AI-driven systems are revolutionizing academic research too.

Imagine being able to access vast databases of information within seconds using natural language processing or predicting trends through machine learning algorithms! So let's turn our attention towards this fascinating frontier: technological advances in academic research that continue to push the boundaries of what's possible for students worldwide every day.

Technological Advances in Academic Research

Imagine being able to dive into a sea of information, pulling out relevant data for your academic projects in an instant using advanced technology. Imagine no more; it's already happening! Thanks to AI tools such as machine learning algorithms and natural language processing, research has become more streamlined than ever.

Now, you're not just part of the crowd trying to make sense of overwhelming data; you're at the forefront, harnessing cutting-edge tech to enhance your study and research efficiency.

With AI-powered tools like content crawlers that can scan hundreds of pages in seconds for relevance or predictive analytics that can identify trends before they emerge, you're no longer on the back foot. You're moving at a faster pace, keeping up with or even surpassing current knowledge in your field.

It's not about isolating yourself behind a screen; it's about connecting with vast resources of information and insights that would have been nearly impossible to gather manually.

The future looks exciting! As these technologies continue to evolve and improve, so will their impact on academic research. The ability to analyze complex datasets quickly and accurately could revolutionize how we approach studies - from hypothesis formulation to data analysis and conclusion drawing.

These advances are carving out a new path where time-consuming tasks become efficient processes, turning mountains into molehills within minutes. Let's ride this wave together as we explore further what lies ahead in 'the future of artificial intelligence in learning and research'.

The Future of Artificial Intelligence in Learning and Research

As we peer into the crystal ball of the future, it's exciting to see how artificial intelligence is poised to reshape learning and academic investigations.

Imagine a world where AI tools can efficiently sort through thousands of research papers, helping you identify trends and patterns that would have taken months, or even years, to uncover manually.

What if these same tools could also help students grasp complex concepts in minutes? The possibilities are endless and thrilling.

Picture yourself being part of an online study group powered by AI. It recognizes your individual strengths and weaknesses, tailoring tutorials specially for you while encouraging collaboration with peers who complement your skills.

You're no longer just studying; you're actively participating in a dynamic learning community where everyone belongs and contributes uniquely. Together with AI, you're not only keeping up with the pace of education but excelling beyond the traditional confines.

Peering further into this promising future, envision sophisticated AI systems taking on more human-like roles in research – conducting experiments based on previous results or suggesting new hypotheses based on emerging data trends.

Researchers won't be replaced; instead they'll be empowered as their time-consuming tasks are automated freeing them up for deeper critical thinking and creative problem-solving.

This isn't some far-off sci-fi dream - it's a glimpse at tomorrow's reality thanks to artificial intelligence's transformative potential in learning and research!

Frequently Asked Questions

What are the potential ethical concerns with the use of AI tools in education and research?

You might worry about the ethical implications of AI in education and research. Issues like user privacy, data security, accuracy of AI-generated content, bias in AI algorithms and unequal access to technology could be concerning.

How can AI tools be integrated into existing learning systems without disrupting traditional teaching methods?

Like adding spices to a dish, integrating AI tools into learning systems can perk up traditional methods. They can be used as supplementary resources, enhancing teaching without usurping the role of educators or disrupting class dynamics.

What are the costs associated with implementing AI tools in educational institutions and research facilities?

While costs can vary, bringing AI tools to your school or lab isn't cheap. You'll face software expenses, hardware upgrades, training costs and maintenance fees. But remember, these investments often lead to priceless outcomes!

What are some of the limitations or drawbacks of using AI tools for enhancing research and studying efficiency?

While AI tools can boost your study efficiency, they're not flawless. They might lack human touch, struggle with complex concepts, and require high initial investment. Moreover, privacy concerns may arise due to data handling practices.

How can AI tools be adapted for use in different fields of study, such as humanities, social sciences, and arts?

Imagine AI as your versatile paintbrush. In humanities, it can analyze texts efficiently. For social sciences, it's adept at examining trends. And in arts, AI can assist in creating and appreciating masterpieces uniquely.

Conclusion

So, you've seen the startling strides AI is making in studying and research realms. Remember, it's not replacing you; rather, it's revolutionizing your role!

Ready or not, rapid advancements are reshaping research and refining learning.

Harness the horsepower of these high-tech tools. Watch as weary weeks of work whittle down to a wink with AI assistance.

Welcome this wonderful wave of change in education and exploration today!

Chapter 8: AI and Finance

AI-Driven Budgeting and Expense Tracking Applications for Better Financial Management

Who hasn't experienced the dilemma of balancing a checkbook or struggled to adhere to a tight budget? Traditional ways of tracking expenses and managing finances can be overwhelming, time-consuming, and sometimes ineffective.

But what if there was an easier way? What if you could leverage the power of artificial intelligence (AI) to make better financial decisions? Well, it's no longer a dream but a reality. AI-driven budgeting and expense tracking apps are here to revolutionize your financial management.

Imagine having a personal finance assistant that not only keeps track of every penny you spend but also analyzes your spending habits, helps set realistic budgets, and predicts future expenditures! It's like having a savvy money manager right in your pocket.

These advanced tools powered by machine learning algorithms offer unparalleled insights into your finances which can ultimately lead to smarter money moves. No more guessing games or being caught off guard by unexpected expenses. With these AI-powered applications in hand, you'll feel more connected and in control of your financial journey.

Key Takeaways

- AI-driven budgeting and expense tracking apps revolutionize financial management by analyzing spending habits, setting realistic budgets, and predicting future expenditures.
- These apps provide unparalleled insights into finances, help visualize where every penny goes, and offer real-time budgeting features with user-friendly charts and graphs.
- Using these tools leads to less stress around money matters, proactive control over personal finances, and informed decisions about trimming down or ramping up expenses based on priorities.
- AI-assisted tools proactively manage money, reduce anxiety related to financial uncertainty, and help plan for the future by analyzing past financial behavior to forecast future spending.

Understanding the Power of Machine Learning in Finances

You'll be amazed at how machine learning can revolutionize your financial management, making budgeting and expense tracking a breeze. Often the thought of managing finances feels like a chore. You have to sift through countless receipts, invoices, and bank statements. Not to mention the grueling task of remembering where every single penny was spent.

However, with AI-driven tools powered by machine learning algorithms, you're no longer alone in this journey. They take on the heavy lifting, sorting out your income and expenses in real-time as they occur.

Imagine being part of a community that embraces technology for financial growth and freedom! These applications don't just track your expenses or create budgets for you. They learn from your spending habits and make smart predictions about future expenditures based on past data trends. This is incredibly beneficial when planning ahead or trying to save up for something special. It's like having a personal finance coach who understands you perfectly - one who knows when you're likely to splurge on coffee or save more during certain times of the year.

Instead of worrying about overspending or forgetting an important bill payment, let these advanced tools do the work for you while providing insightful reports that help improve your money habits over time. With such valuable insights at hand, it's easier than ever before to manage finances effectively without feeling burdened by complex calculations or tedious paperwork tasks anymore.

And beyond just managing today's expenditures with ease, these high-tech applications are setting users up for long-term financial success too.

Let's delve deeper into some specific benefits these advanced financial tools bring into our lives in the next section...

Benefits of Using Advanced Financial Tools

Advanced financial tools can serve as your personal money managers, helping you visualize where every penny goes and revealing spending habits you weren't even aware of. Imagine having a smart assistant on your side that tracks all your expenses, organizes them into categories, and shows you exactly where your money is going. This eye-opening experience could help you identify areas where you're overspending or not saving enough.

These tools use sophisticated AI algorithms to analyze your transaction data, enabling them to spot patterns and trends in your spending behavior that might be invisible to the naked eye.

As part of a community leveraging technology for better financial management, using these advanced applications can provide numerous benefits. For instance, they offer real-time budgeting features so you can monitor your finances on the go. They also provide expense breakdowns in user-friendly charts and graphs making it easier for you to understand your spending habits at a glance. Some even have built-in alerts to notify you when you're nearing or have exceeded budget limits set by yourself - an essential feature for those who struggle with impulse buying or sticking to budgets.

Using these financial tools isn't just about monitoring expenses—it's about gaining insight into how better manage money and improve future financial decisions. They enable proactive control over personal finances which leads to less stress around money matters. And while we've covered many advantages of these AI-driven applications here, remember this is only the beginning of their potential; there are promising innovations on the horizon set to revolutionize personal finance management even further!

With this newfound understanding of the benefits of advanced financial apps, let's now delve deeper into how technology helps analyze one's spending habits more effectively.

Analyzing Your Spending Habits with Technology

Peering into your spending habits with the help of technology is like turning on a flashlight in a dark room, suddenly illuminating areas where money slips away unnoticed. AI-driven budgeting and expense tracking applications serve as that guiding light, helping you understand what happens to every penny you earn.

These intuitive tools not only track your income and expenses but also categorize them for easy analysis. Suddenly, you're no longer guessing or stressing about where your hard-earned money goes; instead, you'll see it all laid out in front of you in an intuitive and user-friendly interface.

These tech-savvy platforms are designed to be more than just digital accountants; they're your personal finance coaches. They provide real-time insights into your spending patterns, showing their impact on your financial goals with striking clarity. You might discover that those morning lattes add up over time or recognize how much eating out drains from your monthly budget.

By unveiling these hidden culprits behind dwindling bank balances, these innovative tools empower you to make informed decisions about where to trim down or ramp up expenses based on priorities.

Through this newfound understanding of your spending behavior, sparked by sophisticated technology, you are better equipped to manage finances effectively. But remember that understanding where money goes is only part of the equation; acting upon this understanding is equally crucial for achieving financial stability.

This leads us naturally towards the importance of setting achievable budgets aided by automated assistance - because when it comes to managing finances smartly, knowledge without action hardly makes any difference at all.

Setting Realistic Budgets with Automated Assistance

Harnessing the power of automated assistance, it's possible to set realistic and achievable budgets that align with your personal financial goals. You're not alone in this journey towards better financial health; AI-driven budgeting apps are here to help you.

They can take into account your income, regular expenses, debt repayments and saving goals before recommending a budget that suits your lifestyle. These applications make it easy for you to understand where your money is going and how you can save more effectively.

Imagine being part of a community where everyone is making informed decisions about their finances, guided by technology. This kind of budgeting isn't just about cutting corners or giving up on things you love; instead, it's about optimizing your finances so you have more freedom and less stress.

With AI-assisted tools, you can proactively manage your money rather than reacting to unexpected expenses after they occur. It's like having a personal finance advisor always at hand who understands and respects your individual needs.

Not only do these tools help with current spending habits and setting realistic budgets but they also predict future expenditures based on past trends - adding another layer of utility to these applications. Imagine knowing what next month's expenses would likely be based on historical data!

This takes the guesswork out of planning for the future, reducing anxiety related to financial uncertainty. Let's delve deeper into how smart algorithms contribute further in predicting future expenditures by understanding our past spending patterns.

Predicting Future Expenditures with Smart Algorithms

Smart algorithms can help you forecast your future spending by analyzing your past financial behavior. For instance, imagine having an intelligent companion who understands your habits thoroughly and uses those insights to guide you towards better financial decisions. When planning a vacation or contemplating a significant purchase, wouldn't it be great if someone could tell you how this expense will influence your future finances?

Well, smart algorithms in AI-driven budgeting apps do just that! They sift through tons of data about your income, recurring expenses, one-time expenditures, and even unexpected costs to give you accurate predictions about what lies ahead.

This level of proactive personal finance management was once only available to large corporations with vast resources. But now, thanks to advancements in artificial intelligence and machine learning techniques, everyone can benefit from these predictive capabilities right from their smartphones! With such tools at our disposal, we're no longer merely reacting to our financial circumstances but actively shaping them.

So go on – embrace the power of smart algorithms in budgeting apps and become part of a community that's taking control of their financial destiny one prediction at a time. Isn't it comforting to know that AI-driven applications are looking out for your financial health?

Frequently Asked Questions

How secure are these AI-driven budgeting and expense tracking applications?

You're in good hands! These AI-driven apps generally have robust security measures, like encryption and multi-factor authentication. You'll feel secure knowing your financial data is protected while you work towards better money management.

What kind of personal or financial information do I need to provide to use these applications?

No need to worry, your security is a priority. Generally, you'll just need to share basic info like income, expenses, and account numbers. By joining us, you're part of a secure financial management community.

Are there any costs or subscription fees associated with these AI-driven budgeting and expense tracking applications?

Absolutely! While some of these savvy budgeting apps are free, others may charge a small subscription fee. You'll find this investment helps you feel in control and part of a community that's mastering their finances.

How user-friendly are these apps for people who are not tech-savvy?

Brilliantly built, these budgeting buddies are user-friendly for everyone. You don't need to be a tech titan to tackle them. They're designed with delight, ensuring even the least tech-savvy users feel part of the digital domain.

Can these applications be used for both personal and business finances?

Absolutely! You're not alone in wanting to streamline both personal and business finances. These applications are designed for you, giving a clear picture of your money matters regardless of their nature or complexity.

Conclusion

So, you see, getting a handle on your finances is like taking a journey. You need the right tools to navigate through the wilderness of bills and expenditures.

AI-driven budgeting apps are your compass in this venture, providing clarity and direction. Don't let financial management intimidate you.

With machine learning by your side, you're better equipped than ever before to track expenses, set realistic budgets, and even predict future spending. Adoption of this technology isn't a luxury anymore; it's a necessity for sound financial health.

AI-Powered Investment Advisors and Stock Market Analysis

You've probably heard the buzzword 'Artificial Intelligence'or AI, right? It's everywhere these days - from your smartphone's voice-activated personal assistant to self-driving cars. But have you ever thought about how it could revolutionize the way you handle your investments and analyze stock market trends? Well, sit back and buckle up as we take you on a journey into the world of AI-powered investment advisors and advanced algorithms designed to predict market trends.

Imagine having a super-smart advisor who never sleeps, tirelessly crunches numbers, and constantly analyzes data patterns in real-time to make optimal investment decisions for you. This isn't science fiction anymore but a reality in today's financial landscape. Big Data is playing an unprecedented role in financial forecasting with machine learning at its core. Under the spotlight is risk analysis and mitigation using technology that can potentially save you from devastating losses. Welcome aboard to the future of finance!

Key Takeaways

- AI-powered investment advisors and advanced algorithms revolutionize investments and stock market analysis.
- Machine learning enables computers to learn from data, identify patterns, and make decisions.
- Big data plays a crucial role in financial forecasting and strategic decision-making.
- AI-powered platforms make complex financial analyses accessible to everyone.

Understanding Machine Learning in Finance

You've probably heard the term 'machine learning' thrown around a lot, but let's really dig into what it means in the world of finance and how it can drastically change your investment strategies.

Machine learning is a subset of Artificial Intelligence (AI) that empowers computers to learn from data, identify patterns, and make decisions with minimal human intervention. In finance, machine learning algorithms are used to predict stock prices, forecast market trends, and even guide investing strategies - all based on historical financial data.

Imagine being part of a team where your computer buddy is crunching numbers at lightning speed and offering you insights that would take humans hours or even days to unravel!

Now that we're all on board with what machine learning brings to the table in finance, let's delve into the benefits it offers you as an investor.

These smart algorithms can analyze vast amounts of financial data quickly and accurately. They help identify profitable investment opportunities by predicting future price movements based on past trends. This level of accuracy often results in higher returns for investors like you!

What's more? You also become part of an exclusive club – those who leverage cutting-edge technology for their financial growth.

Machine learning isn't just about making predictions; it's also about understanding market dynamics at a deeper level. It helps map out complex relationships between various factors influencing stock prices such as company performance metrics, economic indicators, or industry trends.

With this knowledge, you're not only equipped to make better-informed investment decisions but also positioned as an innovator among your peers - someone who embraces technological advancements for personal growth.

So buckle up because this journey with machine learning in finance is only getting started!

Now imagine combining these capabilities with another powerful tool - big data! Let's explore further how this dynamic duo transforms financial forecasting.

The Role of Big Data in Financial Forecasting

Big data's role in financial forecasting can't be underestimated; it provides you with a wealth of detailed insights, allowing you to make more informed and strategic decisions. When you tap into the power of big data, you're not just crunching numbers or following trends - you're unlocking stories hidden within vast amounts of information.

These narratives give you an edge over others who might still be relying on traditional methods for predicting market behavior. You start to become part of a select group that understands how technology is reshaping the investment landscape.

In this tech-driven era where data is king, your ability to analyze and interpret complex datasets can set you apart from the crowd. Imagine being able to predict shifts in market sentiment before they happen, identifying opportunities that others miss, or even mitigating risks before they impact your portfolio. By harnessing big data analytics, you're not just joining the world of AI-powered investing; instead, it's like becoming a member of an exclusive club where everyone speaks the same language - the language of future-ready finance.

As great as this all sounds though, remember it's not just about having access to big data that matters but knowing what to do with it - understanding how these massive volumes of information can inform your strategy and guide your decisions. That's why advanced algorithms play such a crucial role in today's financial forecasting scenario.

They are next in line for discussion as we explore their capacity to predict market trends with unprecedented accuracy.

Predicting Market Trends with Advanced Algorithms

In the pulsating heart of modern finance, advanced algorithms sift through mountains of data, picking up subtle patterns and hidden correlations like a gold miner sieves for precious nuggets. These digital miners work tirelessly to unearth valuable insights that could signal market trends or shifts before they even happen.

It's not magic; it's machine learning - an application of artificial intelligence (AI) that provides systems with the ability to automatically learn and improve from experience without being explicitly programmed. Now, imagine the power you'll wield over your investments when you're able to predict the financial future with precision.

You'll have confidence in your investment decisions because they'll be based on solid data analysis rather than gut feeling. You won't lose sleep over sudden market fluctuations, as predictive algorithms will have already anticipated them and adjusted your portfolio accordingly. The fear of risk will no longer haunt you because AI-driven investment advisors will effectively manage it for you.

It's about belonging to a community of investors who are ahead of their time – those who harness the power of technology not only to maximize their profits but also to minimize their risks. It's about embracing a future where machines work hand-in-hand with humans, bringing forth an era where investing is less about guesswork and more about strategic decision-making driven by hard data.

As we journey further into this brave new world where advanced algorithms reign supreme, we must remember that while these tools are incredibly powerful aids in predicting market trends, they remain just that - tools. They cannot eliminate risk entirely nor guarantee success every time.

This brings us onto a crucial aspect at play here: risk analysis and mitigation using technology can help us navigate around potential pitfalls whilst maximizing our gains from these predictions.

Risk Analysis and Mitigation using Technology

Don't be left in the dust of yesterday's trends; using cutting-edge technology for risk analysis and mitigation is like having a crystal ball that helps you dodge investment landmines while seizing golden opportunities.

Imagine being part of an exclusive club with access to powerful AI tools that accurately predict market volatility, evaluate potential risks, and even suggest strategies to counter them. This isn't just any ordinary club - it's a community where you belong, filled with savvy investors who stay ahead of the curve by embracing innovative solutions.

The beauty of this technological revolution lies not only in its accuracy but also its inclusivity. You don't need to be a Wall Street hotshot or hold an economics degree to harness its power. With user-friendly interfaces and easy-to-understand insights, these AI-powered platforms make complex financial analyses accessible to everyone. It empowers you to manage your investments wisely, mitigate risks effectively, and maximize returns confidently. The sense of belonging comes from knowing you're making informed decisions supported by advanced algorithms and predictive models.

As we delve deeper into the world of artificial intelligence and machine learning in finance management, we can't ignore their significance in shaping our investment strategies. No longer are we bound by traditional constraints or reliant on human intuition alone for decision-making. And as we stand at this exciting crossroads between technology and finance, one can only imagine how automated investment advice will redefine our understanding of wealth management tomorrow.

The Future of Finance: Automated Investment Advice

We're on the brink of a financial revolution, where automated advice promises to shake up how we manage our wealth and make decisions about our money. AI-powered investment advisors are leading this shift, harnessing sophisticated algorithms, machine learning, and vast amounts of data to provide precise, personalized financial guidance at your fingertips.

Imagine having a virtual advisor that knows you as well as you do yourself; understands your risk tolerance, financial goals, and even predicts market trends with uncanny accuracy.

Here's what sets these robo-advisors apart from traditional human counterparts:

- **Personalized Approach:** They use advanced data analytics to understand your unique financial situation.
- **Accessibility:** You have access to financial advice 24/7 without needing an appointment.
- **Affordability:** There's no need for hefty fees or commission rates. These platforms typically charge minimal costs.
- **Efficiency:** No more waiting days for fund transfers or transactions; everything is real-time.

The landscape of finance is changing fast. Automated investment advice isn't just the future - it's here now. So why stick with antiquated methods? Embrace this new era of technology-driven wealth management and imagine what it could mean for you: more control over your investments, lower costs, and potentially better returns than ever before.

The sense of security that comes from knowing that a powerful AI is constantly monitoring the markets on your behalf can be truly liberating. This isn't about replacing human judgment entirely - it's about augmenting it with artificial intelligence to help us all make smarter decisions about our money in an increasingly complex world.

Frequently Asked Questions

What are some of the ethical considerations surrounding the use of AI in financial investments and stock market analysis?

"Ever wondered about fairness in AI financial advice? Ethical concerns include bias in decision-making, lack of transparency, misuse of personal data and the potential for algorithmic errors impacting your hard-earned savings."

How accessible are AI-powered investment advisors to the average individual investor?

You'll be thrilled to know that AI-powered investment advisors are quite accessible! They're becoming increasingly popular, and many platforms cater specifically to individual investors like you. So, you're definitely not left out in the cold.

Can AI-powered investment tools completely replace the need for human financial advisors?

While AI tools can be your loyal sidekick, they can't fully replace human advisors. They lack the personal touch, empathy and intuition a human advisor brings to the table. You need both to navigate investing's rough seas.

How can these AI systems ensure the privacy and security of an individual's financial information?

You're in safe hands! These AI systems prioritize your privacy, using advanced encryption and cybersecurity measures to guard your financial information. They're designed to make you feel secure as part of their community.

How is the effectiveness of these AI-powered investment tools measured and evaluated over time?

Like a maturing wine, the effectiveness of these tech tools is measured over time. They're evaluated based on their prediction accuracy, overall return on investment, risk management resilience, and user satisfaction scores. You're part of this evolution!

Conclusion

You're standing at the dawn of a new era, where machine learning and big data play starring roles in your financial success. It's a world where advanced algorithms can predict market trends and technology helps to mitigate risks.

Imagine this: Your future investments managed by AI-powered advisors, providing you with precise, automated advice. That's not science fiction—it's your financial future made easier and smarter through technology.

Just think about the possibilities!

AI's Role in Detecting and Preventing Fraudulent Activities in Finance

You've probably heard about artificial intelligence (AI) and how it's changing the world, but have you stopped to consider its impact on your finances?

It's more than just self-driving cars and voice-activated assistants. AI is becoming a critical player in the financial sector, particularly in detecting and preventing fraudulent activities. With fraudsters inventing new techniques every day to infiltrate our bank accounts and credit cards, it's reassuring to know that AI has got our back!

Imagine getting an alert from your bank in real-time as a suspicious transaction occurs. Not tomorrow or later today - right now! That's just one of the ways AI is becoming a game changer in financial security.

It's not only saving institutions billions lost through fraud but also giving us peace of mind knowing we're part of a secure community that cares for its members' financial wellbeing. Welcome to the future of finance where you belong; let's explore further how this amazing technology is stepping up against fraudulent activities.

Key Takeaways

- AI plays a critical role in detecting and preventing fraudulent activities in the financial sector.
- High-tech solutions like AI and machine learning algorithms help identify irregular patterns and flag suspicious transactions.
- Real-time fraud prevention powered by AI constantly scans patterns and behaviors to identify fraud, eliminating the need for waiting for monthly statements.
- AI empowers customers by providing enhanced security measures and analyzing billions of transactions each day to identify fraud patterns.

The Rise of Technology in Financial Security

You're now witnessing a significant shift in financial security, as technology's rise has become pivotal in detecting and preventing fraudulent activities. High-tech solutions are reshaping the landscape, making it harder for fraudsters to execute their nefarious plans and easier for businesses to protect themselves and their customers.

You're part of this evolving world where your assets, both personal and professional, have never been safer.

In this digital era, you belong to a community that champions innovation and security. Artificial Intelligence (AI) is the front-runner in these advancements, acting like a guardian angel by identifying irregular patterns or odd transactions that might slip past human detection.

Imagine being part of an ecosystem where your finances are monitored 24/7 by intelligent systems on the lookout for any suspicious activity. That's not just peace of mind; it's being part of something bigger - a secure network powered by smart technology.

So here we are - embracing AI as our ally against fraudsters lurking in the shadows of finance. No longer do we feel helpless against scams or dubious transactions slipping under our radar unnoticed. We've got state-of-the-art tech watching our backs!

And with this newfound confidence, let's delve deeper into exploring how machine learning contributes to fraud detection without missing a beat.

Understanding Machine Learning and Fraud Detection

In the vast universe of banking transactions, it's machine learning that stands as a silent sentinel, tirelessly sifting through data, unmasking deceit hidden in numbers and shielding our hard-earned money from unseen predators. As you go about your business everyday—swiping your card at the coffee shop or transferring funds to a friend—you may not realize the sophisticated technology working behind the scenes.

Machine learning algorithms are continually analyzing patterns, behaviors, and anomalies across millions of transactions globally to ensure that your financial activities remain secure.

You might wonder how this all works? It's really quite fascinating. Let's break it down:

1. **Pattern Recognition**: Machine learning algorithms can identify patterns far more complex than any human could discern. They learn from historical transaction data, identifying normal behavior for each individual user and flagging anything unusual.

2. **Anomaly Detection**: The algorithm is designed to detect any deviation from the usual pattern as a potential threat. This could include an unusually large purchase, an odd transaction location, or even something as subtle as a different time of transaction.

3. **Predictive Analysis**: Perhaps most impressively, machine learning can predict future fraud attempts based on past activity and trends.

Despite its complexities, understanding machine learning doesn't have to feel like you're trying to unravel some arcane secret society's codebook. Instead, think of it as having your own personal bodyguard who never sleeps—always vigilant and equipped with the best tools technology has to offer.

Preparing for threats before they occur is becoming increasingly crucial in today's fast-paced digital world where real-time fraud prevention is no longer a luxury but an absolute necessity—a game changer indeed!

Real-time Fraud Prevention: A Game Changer

Isn't it comforting to know that every single time you make a transaction, there's an advanced technology working tirelessly to shield your finances from the unknown dangers lurking in the digital world? Real-time fraud prevention, powered by AI and machine learning, is this game-changing technology.

It's constantly scanning patterns and behaviors, identifying pesky anomalies that could signal fraudulent activity. This means that before anything suspicious has a chance to affect your account or transactions, it's already been spotted and halted. You're part of a community being guarded 24/7 against financial predators.

Imagine if we were stuck in the old days – waiting for monthly statements to arrive just to comb through them for any irregularities or discrepancies. Not only would this be time-consuming, but also ineffective in catching frauds quickly enough. But now, with real-time fraud detection on our side, those worries are things of the past! In fact, it feels like you have a personal detective committed to safeguarding your financial health round-the-clock. We all belong together in this era where security feels less like an afterthought and more like a built-in feature.

This transformative approach isn't just beneficial for us as individuals; it also brings tremendous advantages for financial institutions themselves. By reducing false positives and improving accuracy in detecting genuine threats, they can maintain trust with their customers - that's us - while keeping operational costs down. After all, who wouldn't want a bank that not only understands their needs but goes above and beyond to protect their hard-earned money?

Now let's delve deeper into how these advancements are reshaping relationships between banks and their customers...

Impact on Financial Institutions and Customers

Advancements in real-time fraud prevention have undeniably revolutionized the dynamics between financial institutions and their clientele. Not only has it changed how banks operate, but it's also dramatically improved your experience as a customer.

With AI at the helm of detecting and preventing fraudulent activities, you can rest easy knowing that your money is safer than ever before. You no longer have to fear those horror stories of waking up one morning to find your savings wiped out by some faceless scammer halfway across the globe.

As a valued consumer, this development empowers you with greater control over your finances. The AI systems are tirelessly working behind-the-scenes, analyzing billions of transactions each day to identify patterns that could signify fraud. So if something suspicious pops up on your account - like an unusually large transaction or activity from an unfamiliar location – the system flags it instantly. This means less time spent worrying about potential threats and more time enjoying the peace of mind that comes with secure finances.

As we delve deeper into this digital age, remember that these advancements aren't just about making life easier; they're about creating a sense of community where everyone feels protected and taken care of. Enhanced security measures don't just benefit individual customers; they uplift entire institutions by fostering trust and confidence in their services.

As we look toward 'the future of security in the financial sector', let's not forget our shared journey towards this milestone and continue striving for a world where everyone can feel truly secure in their financial dealings.

The Future of Security in the Financial Sector

You might think that the financial world is bulletproof, but ironically, there's never been a time when it's more vulnerable - yet simultaneously safer - thanks to cutting-edge security measures.

As we launch into the future of finance, AI technology plays an increasingly central role in ensuring our transactions are secure and our data remains private. Despite the sophistication of fraudsters and cybercriminals, AI has become an indispensable ally in detecting potential fraudulent activity before it wreaks havoc on individuals and institutions alike.

The future seems promising with numerous advancements in AI-led security systems. Increased use of biometric identification methods such as facial recognition and fingerprint scanning will make it harder for unauthorized users to gain access to sensitive information. Coupled with machine learning algorithms, these technologies can continually adapt and improve their detection capabilities.

The development of predictive analytics techniques powered by AI can identify unusual patterns or behaviors that could signify fraudulent activities. These intelligent systems not only monitor transactions but also learn from them, enabling proactive prevention instead of reactive damage control.

As you navigate this futuristic landscape where tech-enhanced safety is no longer a privilege but a necessity, remember that your role is crucial too. Stay vigilant about sharing personal information online, routinely update your passwords – yes, even those pesky ones which seem impossible to remember – while also being open-minded about embracing new authentication measures like biometrics for added security layers.

While the world may be becoming more susceptible to threats lurking in cyber shadows, take comfort knowing that an army of AIs is tirelessly working behind the scenes protecting us all from potential financial harm. Remember — you're not alone in this fight against fraudulent activity; we're all part of this shared journey towards greater financial security secured by artificial intelligence.

Frequently Asked Questions

What is the cost of implementing AI technology for fraud detection in financial institutions?

The cost of implementing AI for fraud detection can vary greatly. It depends on your institution's size, the complexity of your operations, and the specific AI solutions you choose. But remember, it's a worthy investment!

How does AI's role in fraud detection compare to traditional methods?

"Old dogs can learn new tricks, especially with AI in fraud detection. It's more efficient, faster, and accurate than traditional methods. With AI, you're part of a smarter community that's one step ahead of fraudsters."

What are the potential risks or challenges of using AI for fraud detection in finance?

While AI can boost fraud detection, it's not foolproof. The risks include false positives, which can annoy customers. Also, hackers might outsmart the system or use its learning capabilities for their own nefarious purposes.

Are there specific examples of financial institutions that have successfully used AI for fraud detection and prevention?

Sure, you've heard of PayPal, right? They're like the sheriffs of the digital wild west. Their AI systems scan millions of transactions daily, successfully detecting and preventing fraudulent activity. You're not alone in this fight!

Can AI technology completely eliminate the risk of fraudulent activities in the financial sector?

While AI technology greatly reduces fraud risk, it can't entirely eliminate it. Like you, even the most sophisticated systems can be fooled by innovative scams. But don't worry, it's getting better every day!

Conclusion

You're living in a fantastic era where technology like AI is reshaping finance, making it more secure and efficient. It's not just about convenience anymore; it's about your hard-earned money being protected from fraudsters.

Imagine this: you're shopping online when suddenly, a suspicious transaction alert pops up on your phone. It's AI working behind the scenes to keep your finances safe. Who knows? The future could hold even more amazing tech advancements for financial security.

Chapter 9: AI in Travel and Exploration

AI-Driven Travel Planning Apps for Seamless Trip Organization and Booking

Navigating the labyrinth of travel planning can feel like trying to solve a Rubik's cube in the dark. It's a jigsaw puzzle where every piece - from booking flights and hotels, researching destinations, arranging transportation, to drafting itineraries - needs to fit perfectly together.

But what if you had a digital assistant who could illuminate that darkness and put all the pieces in place with ease? What if technology could transform your travel planning process into an effortless adventure?

In this fast-paced world where time is as precious as gold dust, AI-driven travel planning apps are stepping onto center stage as your personal travel agents. These intelligent tools are all about creating seamless trip organization and booking experiences tailor-made just for you. They're not just cutting-edge; they're revolutionizing how we plan our vacations, turning tedious tasks into simple steps that even the most tech-averse individuals can enjoy.

Just imagine having your own personal genie at your beck and call, ready to make your travel dreams come true!

Key Takeaways

- AI-driven travel planning apps revolutionize trip organization and booking by providing personalized solutions based on user preferences and past behavior.
- These apps utilize predictive analysis to accurately predict future travel trends, helping with budget management, itinerary creation, and booking accommodations and transport.
- They offer real-time updates on flight prices and suggest offbeat attractions, while also providing comprehensive dashboard features for organizing tickets and hotel bookings.
- AI-driven travel planning apps simplify travel planning, enhance personalization, and create unique adventures tailored to individual preferences, replacing paper maps, language barriers, and random hotel bookings.

The Rise of Digital Assistance in Vacation Planning

There's no denying it, the rise of digital assistance in vacation planning has revolutionized how we organize and book our trips! Gone are the days when you had to juggle multiple tabs on your browser, cross-referencing hotel costs with flight prices. Now, AI-driven apps take all that hard work off your hands. They not only find the best deals for you but also make sure everything fits seamlessly into your schedule.

It's like having a personal travel agent who knows exactly what you want and need!

In this tech-savvy world where everyone craves convenience and efficiency, these apps really make a difference. You're part of a global community that values smart solutions for everyday tasks—and trip planning is no exception. This shift towards digital assistance isn't just about saving time or money; it's about being part of a movement that embraces technology to enhance our lives in meaningful ways.

So, as you navigate through this ever-evolving landscape of vacation planning tools, remember: these aren't just impersonal algorithms at work. They're intelligent software systems designed with your needs in mind. These AI-driven tools can adapt to your preferences over time—learning from past trips to better cater to future ones—a truly personalized experience!

As we dive deeper into understanding their capabilities next, remember they're not just here to help plan vacations; they're reshaping our experiences and redefining how we belong in this digital era.

Understanding the Capabilities of Intelligent Software

With a touch of suspense, let's delve into the world of intelligent software, where you'll be astounded by its capabilities. Imagine yourself planning a trip; instead of hopping from one website to another, comparing prices and making reservations, an AI-driven travel app handles all these tasks for you. It not only finds the best deals but also plans your itinerary based on your preferences and past behavior. It's like having a personal assistant who knows you inside out!

Now, imagine this: You're sitting in your living room sipping coffee, and suddenly you get a notification from your AI travel app about an upcoming art exhibition in Paris that aligns with your interests. Not only that, but it has also found an affordable round-trip ticket for you during the exhibit dates! This is what we mean when we talk about 'intelligent' software. It's not just about automation; it's about understanding user needs on a granular level and providing personalized solutions.

Don't think of this as some distant future technology; it's here now. The capability to make informed decisions based on patterns detected in user data sets these apps apart from traditional travel platforms. They're designed to make our lives more convenient by handling complex tasks with ease and precision – much like how a friend would help us plan our trips by knowing our likes and dislikes to create the perfect vacation experience!

Now that we've seen what these smart apps can do, let's move onto selecting the right tool that will cater perfectly to your unique travel desires.

Choosing the Best Tool for Your Needs

Selecting an ideal tool tailored to your specific needs can indeed elevate your vacationing experience to a whole new level of personalization and convenience. With the multitude of AI-driven travel planning apps available, making the right choice might seem daunting at first. But don't worry! By identifying your unique travel preferences and requirements, you'll find an app that's not just user-friendly but also feels like it was custom-made for you.

When scouting for the perfect tool, consider factors like budget management, itinerary creation, accommodation and transport booking features. Do you want real-time updates on flight prices? Or perhaps an app that suggests offbeat attractions based on your interests? Maybe you're someone who likes everything organized neatly in one place - from tickets to hotel bookings. If so, look for apps with comprehensive dashboard features. Remember, the best AI-driven travel planning app is one that makes you feel part of a global community of travelers while offering personalized recommendations.

As you delve deeper into these technologically advanced tools, get ready to uncover their true potential through predictive analysis. These AI-powered platforms are equipped with algorithms capable of predicting future trends based on historical data and current patterns - all designed to provide you with a seamless trip organization and booking experience. Next up: let's explore how we can harness this power of predictive analysis for smarter traveling decisions!

Harnessing the Power of Predictive Analysis

Imagine having the ability to foresee trends and changes in your vacation plans - that's the magic of predictive analysis at your fingertips! It's like getting a sneak peek into tomorrow, today.

With AI-driven travel planning apps powered by predictive analytics, you can anticipate hitches even before they occur. These tools analyze past and current data patterns to make highly accurate predictions about what's likely to happen in the future. As such, they help you stay one step ahead of any eventuality, ensuring nothing comes between you and your perfect getaway.

- You'll have a better understanding of when flight prices are likely to drop or soar; no more guesswork!
- You can predict weather conditions for your chosen dates so you'll know exactly what to pack.
- Get insights on the best times to visit popular tourist hotspots based on crowd predictions.
- Be prepared for potential disruptions by predicting peak travel seasons or possible events that might affect your trip.
- Predictive analysis helps align your preferences with optimal booking options; no more settling!

Now picture yourself making all these informed decisions effortlessly from one app interface – pretty impressive, right?

The power of this technology isn't just in its forecasting abilities but also how it enhances personalization. It understands not just where you want to go but also how you want to experience it based on past behaviors and preferences. Henceforth, every journey becomes a unique adventure tailored precisely for you.

As we navigate through this exciting era filled with technological innovations that simplify our lives, remember that these aren't mere software features but tools designed for connection and convenience. They're here not only to make travel planning less daunting but also create memorable experiences worth cherishing forever.

So let's gear up as we delve deeper into how technology continues enhancing our travel experiences beyond imagination!

Enhancing Your Travel Experience Through Technology

Isn't it astonishing how technology has revolutionized our travel experiences? The days of paper maps, language barriers, and random hotel bookings are a thing of the past. Now, with AI-driven travel planning apps at your fingertips, organizing and booking your trip has never been easier or more seamless.

You belong to an era where convenience isn't just desired but expected - technology ensures that you get just that. Imagine having a personal assistant who does all the tedious work for you – researching destinations, comparing prices, finding the best places to eat and visit; all tailored to your preferences. That's exactly what these innovative apps do for you! They utilize advanced algorithms and predictive analytics to provide personalized recommendations based on your likes and dislikes.

Whether you're a history buff seeking culturally rich locations or an adventure junkie looking for adrenaline-pumping activities, there's something for everyone! The beauty of this tech-driven approach extends beyond mere convenience; it enhances every aspect of your journey from start to finish.

From real-time updates about flight delays or cancellations straight to your device, interactive maps guiding you through unfamiliar cities like a local expert would do, translating foreign languages in real-time so no communication barrier can stand in your way; everything works harmoniously together helping create unforgettable memories from every adventure undertaken.

So why wait? Embrace this wave of digital transformation in travel planning today and be part of the global community experiencing smarter travels!

Frequently Asked Questions

What are the potential privacy concerns when using AI-driven travel planning apps?

When using AI-driven travel apps, you might worry about your personal data. They often require access to sensitive information like location, preferences, and potentially your payment details - a potential goldmine for cybercriminals.

Can these travel planning apps handle unexpected changes or cancellations?

Surely, savvy software swiftly steps in when surprises strike. These travel tools take the hassle out of hasty changes or cancellations, creating a comforting community of carefree commuters confident in their constantly changing plans.

How often are these AI-driven travel planning apps updated with new features?

"Updates for these travel planning apps roll out regularly, darling! Developers are always on their toes, adding cool new features. So you'll constantly feel part of a community that's evolving and improving together. How exciting!"

Are there any subscription fees or hidden costs associated with these apps?

Did you know 80% of travel apps are free? However, some might have in-app purchases or subscription plans. So, you're part of the savvy majority who love exploring without hidden costs. No surprise fees here!

Is offline functionality available for these AI-based travel planning apps?

Absolutely! You're never alone with these apps. Even offline, they'll be your trusty companions, guiding you through unknown territories. No need for data or Wi-Fi - your travel plans are always on hand.

Conclusion

So, you've uncovered the power of AI in travel planning. It's not just about booking flights and hotels anymore; it's about personalizing your entire journey. You're no longer a passive player but an active one, shaping your experiences through technology. Embrace the predictive analysis, let it guide you to undiscovered places and new adventures. With the right app in hand, you're not just planning a trip - you're curating unforgettable memories. AI is indeed revolutionizing how we travel!

AI-Powered Language Translation for Smoother Communication during Travels

Imagine you're traveling in a foreign country, surrounded by unfamiliar sounds of an unknown language. You're trying to ask for directions, but no one seems to understand your words. It's frustrating and isolating, isn't it?

Now imagine having a tool at your disposal that can instantly translate your words into the local language, breaking down barriers and fostering connections with people around the world. This is not just a figment of imagination anymore - thanks to artificial intelligence (AI).

With AI-powered translation tools, you don't have to feel like an outsider when travelling abroad. These smart devices use machine learning algorithms to learn new languages and phrases from vast amounts of data quickly and accurately. They offer real-time translations that help bridge communication gaps, making travel experiences smoother than ever before.

So whether you're ordering food in Paris or bargaining in Bangkok's bustling markets, these AI translators are set to become your best travel companion!

Key Takeaways

- AI-powered language translation tools break down language barriers and foster connections in foreign countries.
- These tools use machine learning algorithms to provide real-time translations that adapt and improve over time.
- They are able to handle idiomatic expressions, understand context, grammar, nuances, and slang, and provide accurate translations as they process more data.
- AI-powered language translation enhances the travel experience by improving communication, promoting inclusivity and belonging, and facilitating cultural exchange and understanding.

The Rise of Technology in Overcoming Language Barriers

Imagine you're in a bustling foreign market, the air filled with unfamiliar sounds and words. Suddenly, your smartphone becomes your personal translator, effortlessly breaking down language barriers and transforming your travel experience. You're no longer an outsider struggling to communicate; instead, you're part of the vibrant scene unfolding around you.

With every interaction made seamless by technology, you feel more connected to this foreign land than ever before. You see, technology has grown leaps and bounds over the past few years, ushering in a new era where language is no longer an obstacle but an opportunity for deeper understanding and connection. AI-powered translation tools have changed how we interact and connect with people from different cultures.

No need to worry about miscommunication or misunderstandings when asking for directions or ordering food at local eateries anymore - these smart apps are there for you like a friendly local guide who speaks your tongue! They not only help decode foreign languages but also bring us closer together as global citizens in our increasingly interconnected world.

So next time when you pack your bags to explore that exotic destination on your bucket list, remember to take along this digital companion that will ensure smoother communication during travels. Just imagine how much richer your traveling experiences could be if understanding the local language wasn't a hurdle anymore!

And speaking of understanding languages better - isn't it fascinating how these nifty translation tools work? Let's delve deeper into their inner workings: specifically their use of machine learning to provide accurate translations.

Understanding Machine Learning in Translation Tools

Diving into the intriguing world of machine learning, let's explore how this advanced technology is revolutionizing translation tools and erasing language barriers in a snap. Machine learning, a subset of artificial intelligence, enables computers to learn from data without being explicitly programmed. In the context of translation tools, these systems analyze massive amounts of text in different languages and gradually improve their ability to translate accurately by recognizing patterns and making connections.

Machine learning can handle idiomatic expressions which are often challenging for traditional translators.

Translation tools with machine learning capabilities adapt over time, becoming more accurate as they work through more translations.

These AI-powered solutions can provide instantaneous translations, allowing for seamless communication even when you don't speak the local language.

Now imagine yourself walking down the streets of an unfamiliar city abroad. You're trying to communicate with locals but there's a language barrier. Suddenly your phone comes to the rescue! All you have to do is type or speak what you want to say into your device and voila - a precise translation appears right before your eyes! That's machine learning at its finest: constantly improving itself based on new information it encounters. The beauty lies not just in its powerful functionality but also in the sense of belonging it fosters as you navigate foreign lands without feeling lost or excluded because of language differences.

As we continue our journey through this fascinating technological landscape, we'll next delve into another critical aspect that has significantly augmented real-time translation - artificial intelligence (AI). But hold on tight, because as impressive as machine-learning-assisted translations may be, AI takes it up a notch by offering even further advancements in breaking down language barriers during travels.

The Role of Artificial Intelligence in Real-Time Translation

You've likely marveled at the speed and accuracy of real-time translation, but have you ever wondered what makes it all possible? Spoiler alert: It's artificial intelligence! AI has become a linchpin in the world of instantaneous translation, ensuring that language is no longer a barrier in our globalized society.

From your favorite travel apps to subtitled foreign films, the magic behind this seamless communication is pure AI wizardry.

AI-powered translation tools use complex algorithms and machine learning to understand context, grammar, nuances, or even slang. They're not just swapping words from one language to another; they're understanding language patterns and translating them correctly into another tongue.

What's more exciting is that these systems learn over time. The more data they process, the better they get at providing accurate translations. Imagine being part of an international community where everyone can communicate without any linguistic barriers - now isn't that an exciting prospect?

But let's face it; there's nothing quite like exploring new places around the globe as smoothly as if you were a local speaking their dialect fluently. Thanks to AI innovations in real-time translations, this dream has become a reality for many travelers worldwide.

Stay tuned for how these advancements are making globe-trotting experiences richer than ever before!

Benefits for Global Travelers

Did you know that nearly 76% of global travelers who used real-time translation tools reported a significant improvement in their overall travel experience? Yes, you heard it right. Having access to AI-powered language translation can dramatically enhance your trip, making it more enjoyable and less stressful.

No more struggling with menus or asking for directions in a foreign language. Just imagine how liberating this could be! You'd be able to navigate any city like a local, understand the culture better, and even make friends along the way.

Moreover, these advanced tools aren't just about convenience; they're also about connection. By breaking down language barriers, they empower us to build bridges with people from all walks of life. They allow us to share experiences, stories, and laughter without being hindered by linguistic differences. Isn't that what travel is all about? After all, we're social creatures who crave connections and shared experiences.

With each passing day, technology continues to evolve at an exponential pace - transforming our lives in ways we never thought possible before now. Especially when it comes to facilitating smoother communication during travels through AI-powered translations.

Imagine no longer needing phrase books or awkward hand gestures to communicate while traveling abroad! And as exciting as these developments are now - just think about what the future holds! This is merely a glimpse into tomorrow's world where fluency won't be bound by one's birthplace but enabled through innovative tech solutions such as AI-powered translators.

Future Trends in AI and Language Translations

Looking ahead, it's thrilling to see the potential for advancements in artificial intelligence and linguistic technology that promise to revolutionize how we interact with others globally.

Imagine a world where language barriers no longer dictate your travel destinations or business ventures. AI-powered translation devices could soon become as ubiquitous as smartphones, making global communication more seamless than ever before. These sophisticated tools can provide real-time translations, even picking up on cultural nuances and idioms that usually get lost in translation.

As you navigate through foreign lands, picture yourself equipped with an AI companion capable of translating any language into your own instantly. This isn't some distant sci-fi dream; it's a reality that's unfolding right now!

Tech giants are already experimenting with advanced neural networks designed to understand and translate multiple languages at once. And there's something incredibly unifying about this prospect - it means you're never really alone or out of place when exploring new cultures or forging international relationships.

Pushing beyond just words and phrases, one of the exciting future trends is towards 'emotional' translations – interpreting tone, sarcasm, humor – adding a whole new dimension to the way we communicate across different languages.

The possibilities are endless: You could have nuanced conversations with locals while backpacking through remote villages; negotiate complex business deals overseas without fear of misunderstanding; even watch foreign movies exactly as they were intended without relying on subtitles!

As these technologies improve and become more accessible, they signal a future where everyone can feel like they belong, anywhere in the world.

Frequently Asked Questions

What are the primary languages that AI translation tools can currently handle?

Just like a well-traveled linguist, you'll find AI translation tools adept at handling a myriad of languages. From English, Spanish and French to Mandarin, Japanese and Arabic, they've got the globe covered.

How reliable is AI language translation in comparison to a human translator?

While AI language translation has made leaps, it's not quite on par with human translators yet. It can sometimes miss nuances or cultural context that a human naturally grasps. But it's getting better every day!

Are there any notable drawbacks or limitations of using AI for language translation?

Just like Achilles had his heel, AI translators have their flaws too. They may struggle with nuances, cultural references, and dialects. These limitations could leave you feeling a bit lost in translation sometimes.

How does AI-powered language translation handle regional dialects and accents?

AI-powered translation tools are getting increasingly adept at handling regional dialects and accents. They're learning from vast amounts of data, enabling you to understand local nuances that enrich your conversations and connections.

Can AI translation tools work offline or do they always require an internet connection?

Like a desert without rain, your translation tool may feel barren offline. But fear not, some AI translation tools can indeed work offline. They'll keep you connected even when the world wide web isn't within reach.

Conclusion

So, you see, AI-powered translation tools are the secret weapon in your travel arsenal. They break down walls of miscommunication, building bridges to seamless interaction no matter where you wander.

The future looks bright for globetrotters like you. With advancements in AI and machine learning, it won't be long before language barriers become as antiquated as a rotary dial phone!

So gear up for an era of smoother communication during travels.

Virtual Travel Experiences and AI-Guided Explorations of New Destinations

Ever dreamt of exploring the ancient ruins of Rome, or strolling down the bustling streets of Tokyo, all from the comfort of your own home? Well, you're not alone. As technology continues to evolve and reshape our world, it's also changing the way we experience travel.

Today, with a blend of virtual reality (VR) and artificial intelligence (AI), globetrotting has taken on an entirely new dimension - welcome to the era of digital tourism.

Imagine being able to tour exotic locations without worrying about flight bookings, accommodation or even jet lag. AI-powered virtual tours are offering just that— immersive experiences tailored specifically for you. But that isn't all; these tech-driven explorations allow you to connect with diverse cultures and places in ways that traditional travel might never offer.

So buckle up as we journey into this exciting frontier where technology meets wanderlust.

Key Takeaways

- Virtual travel experiences offer immersive and realistic sightseeing without the need for physical travel.
- AI-powered tour guidance personalizes itineraries based on individual interests, analyzing past trips, preferences, and social media likes.
- Virtual reality combined with AI algorithms will customize virtual tours based on individual tastes and interests, revolutionizing travel experiences.
- Virtual travel allows for exploration of previously inaccessible locations, creating a sense of connection and belonging.

The Rise of Digital Tourism

You're living in an exciting era where digital tourism is on the rise, letting you explore new destinations right from your couch. Can't travel to Paris or Tokyo due to time constraints or budget restrictions? No problem! Now, with a click of a button, you can wander around the Eiffel Tower or stroll through Shibuya Crossing.

You no longer need to feel left out when your friends discuss their latest adventures; you too are part of this global community of explorers.

Virtual tourism has provided a sense of belonging like never before. Not only does it allow for exploration without leaving home, but it also fosters connections with people all over the world. Imagine sitting at home and engaging in meaningful conversations with locals in Greece, sharing stories and experiences as if you were there physically. It's not just about seeing places; it's about experiencing them culturally and socially - becoming part of a larger global narrative.

As amazing as virtual travel is, believe it or not, things are getting even more immersive! The next frontier lies beyond computer screens and mobile devices; we're talking about total immersion into foreign environments right from your living room. This is where virtual reality comes in - offering sightseeing experiences that feel so real you'd swear you could smell the croissants baking in Parisian bakeries.

But more on that when we dive deeper into 'Immersive Sightseeing With Virtual Reality'.

Immersive Sightseeing with Virtual Reality

Immerse yourself in the stunning landscapes and soak up the rich history of far-off places - all from the comfort of your living room. Imagine standing on top of the Great Wall of China, feeling the cool breeze blow through your hair as you gaze upon miles and miles of majestic stone snaking across lush green hills.

Or plunge into the deep blue waters off Australia's Great Barrier Reef, surrounded by a kaleidoscope of colorful coral and myriad marine life. Thanks to virtual reality (VR), these immersive sightseeing experiences are now only a headset away.

With VR technology, you're not just observing a destination; you're virtually transported there. You can roam around centuries-old castles in Europe or walk along serene beaches in Bali without leaving your home. This isn't about replacing physical travel but enriching it; creating connections between you and places that might be thousands of miles away yet feels incredibly close thanks to high-definition 360-degree visuals and lifelike sound effects that give a whole new meaning to armchair traveling.

These immersive virtual tours wouldn't be possible without artificial intelligence (AI) stepping into play. AI enhances VR experiences by rendering realistic environments based on photos and videos, which heightens your sense of presence within the virtual world. It allows for personalized tour guidance based on your interests – maybe it's art history or local cuisine – making each journey uniquely yours.

So as we dive deeper into exploring how AI further elevates these incredible digital adventures, remember this: with VR tourism powered by AI, every corner of our beautiful globe is just a click away!

The Role of Artificial Intelligence in Tour Guidance

Imagine the thrill of discovering hidden gems and secret spots in a foreign city, all tailored to your unique tastes and interests, thanks to the power of artificial intelligence. AI technology is transforming the way we travel by offering personalized tour guidance that goes beyond conventional travel brochures or standard city tours.

It can analyze your past trips, preferences, and even social media likes to curate an itinerary that suits you best. So whether you're a foodie wanting to try local delicacies, or a history buff interested in heritage sites, AI has got you covered.

Think about this: Your guide is not just any guide but an intelligent system designed with algorithms that learn from your behavior. It recommends places based on what it knows you will enjoy and not simply what's popular or highly-rated. You get to explore at your own pace without worrying about keeping up with a group or missing out on anything because everything is customized for you.

With AI as your personal tour guide, there's no limit to how deeply connected you can feel with the destinations you visit. Instead of following a one-size-fits-all approach, each journey becomes an intimate exploration where every turn holds potential for new discoveries uniquely suited for you. This is more than just sightseeing; it's creating meaningful connections through shared experiences with cultures around the world right from your living room.

This digital exploration doesn't stop at customizing travel plans but extends into making these immersive virtual reality experiences accessible anytime anywhere. And while nothing can replace physically being in a new place soaking up its atmosphere firsthand, exploring digitally offers benefits worth uncovering in our next discussion.

Benefits of Exploring Digitally

While it's true that there's no place like home, taking a digital leap can offer advantages akin to Dorothy stepping into the technicolor world of Oz.

Imagine waking up and instead of being confined to your usual surroundings, you're suddenly exploring the depths of the Great Barrier Reef or wandering through the vibrant streets of Tokyo - all from your living room couch.

Virtual travel grants you access to far-flung places without requiring physical movement; it's an escape hatch that opens up new worlds for exploration right at your fingertips.

Engaging in these AI-guided journeys not only quenches your thirst for adventure but also creates a sense of belonging, weaving an intricate web connecting you with people and cultures worldwide.

You get to interact with locals as if you are actually there, share their stories and experience their traditions.

You become part of a global community without leaving your comfort zone – expanding horizons while deepening connections.

The rewards extend beyond just emotional satisfaction too.

Digital explorations save time and resources by eliminating travel costs and reducing environmental impact—no more worrying about flight emissions or over-tourism ruining pristine locations.

As we look towards a future where technology continues to break barriers, these virtual adventures promise us an exciting transformation in how we perceive tourism altogether.

The Future of Tourism Industry

In the not-so-distant future, we'll see a seismic shift in tourism as digital leaps and bounds redefine our concept of exploration. Imagine swapping your suitcase for your sofa,

Are there any negative effects or risks associated with the prolonged use of VR technology for virtual travel?

Absolutely, prolonged VR usage can lead to eye strain, dizziness, and even balance issues. It's essential to take regular breaks, ensuring you're not losing touch with reality while exploring those fascinating digital worlds.

Is there any scope for interactive or multiplayer features in these AI-guided virtual tours?

Absolutely! Imagine exploring a virtual realm with your friends, just like a band of explorers. AI-guided tours can indeed offer multiplayer features, bringing together folks from different corners for a shared adventure.

Conclusion

In this brave new world, you're not just a bystander. You're an explorer, charting your path through digital landscapes as easily as turning the pages of a book.

The future of tourism is like an unwritten novel, and with AI-guided virtual travel experiences at your fingertips, you're the author.

So dive in and embrace the journey! Remember, it's not about reaching a destination - it's about immersing yourself in the adventure that technology offers.

Chapter 10: AI and Social Impact

AI's Potential to Address Societal Challenges, Such As Poverty, Healthcare Accessibility, and Education Gaps

Imagine a world where no one goes to bed hungry, where every kid has access to quality education, and everyone can afford medical services.

Picture the power of technology, specifically Artificial Intelligence (AI), being leveraged to bridge the gap between the haves and have-nots. It's not just a dream; it's an achievable reality that could be closer than you think.

You're part of this future – a society where we use AI to tackle some of our most pressing issues head-on. From economic disparity to healthcare accessibility and educational gaps, artificial intelligence holds the potential to revolutionize how we approach these challenges.

You are at the forefront of this transformation - whether as an innovator, decision-maker or even as an informed citizen understanding its implications.

So let's dive into this brave new world together and discover how AI is reshaping our societal landscape for the better.

Key Takeaways
- AI has the potential to bridge the gap between the haves and have-nots in terms of hunger, education, and medical services.
- AI-powered services and ethical AI development can contribute to reducing poverty.
- AI can democratize healthcare by providing virtual consultations, personalized health assistance, and advanced analysis of symptoms and diagnoses.
- AI can revolutionize education by creating personalized learning plans and providing emotional support.

Tackling Economic Disparity through Machine Learning

Machine learning's potential isn't just about boosting business profits; it's also a powerful tool we can leverage to tackle economic disparity head-on. It's like having an ally that never sleeps, tirelessly working to level the playing field for everyone.

From identifying employment opportunities in underserved communities, optimizing resource allocation for social programs, to predicting economic trends that inform policy decisions - machine learning is our steadfast partner in making a more equitable world.

You're part of this exciting journey too! Every time you use a service powered by AI or support businesses that invest in ethical AI development, you're helping build an economy where everyone gets their fair share. Imagine being able to say 'I played my part in reducing poverty' because every small action, when combined with the efforts of others across the globe, can bring about significant change.

Machine learning models are only as good as the data they're trained on and your interaction with AI-powered services contributes valuable information that helps these models understand and address income inequality better.

Isn't it thrilling how we could utilize technology not just for personal gain but also as an instrument for societal progress? And guess what? That's not all machine learning has up its sleeve! The same principles of pattern recognition and predictive analysis that help us fight financial inequity have another exciting application: addressing healthcare disparities.

So let's delve into how intelligent systems are bridging the divide in medical services next.

Bridging the Divide in Medical Services with Intelligent Systems

Harnessing the power of intelligent systems, we're on the brink of a medical revolution that could bridge the divide in medical services, transforming how we diagnose and treat illnesses. Artificial Intelligence (AI) brings more than just an upgrade—it promises to democratize healthcare, turning what was once exclusive into something accessible for everyone.

Picture this: you're living in a remote area with limited access to healthcare facilities—sounds daunting, right? But with AI advancements, not anymore.

Imagine the possibilities:

- You can have virtual consultations with top-notch doctors from around the world at any time.
- AI-powered apps become your personal health assistants, helping monitor vital signs or remind you about medication.
- Advanced algorithms can analyze your symptoms and provide potential diagnoses based on vast databases of medical knowledge.
- Machine learning models could predict health risks before they become serious issues.
- And lastly, imagine having personalized treatment plans designed by AI using data from thousands of similar cases.

Doesn't it sound like a future where everyone gets a fair shot at quality healthcare? It isn't just about improving efficiency but fostering inclusivity. AI is not merely technology; it's our partner in making sure everyone feels seen and cared for.

As we look forward to these exciting prospects in healthcare accessibility made possible by AI, let's remember—progress doesn't stop here. It only paves the way for even more transformative changes across other sectors too.

Imagine classrooms teeming with digital intelligence—a scenario where every child has their personalized tutor guiding them through their educational journey. Let's delve deeper into how AI is reinventing education next!

Transforming Learning Environments with Digital Intelligence

Isn't it thrilling to envision a future where every child, regardless of their background, can have their learning journey tailored just for them by the power of digital intelligence?

Imagine a world where AI takes an active and helpful role in shaping our education system. Being able to create personalized learning plans based on each student's strengths, weaknesses, interests, and pace of learning could revolutionize the way we approach education. It could break down barriers to achievement and open up opportunities for all children, whether they're from a disadvantaged urban neighborhood or a high-end suburban school district.

Now imagine this: AI doesn't only play the role of an academic guide but also as an empathetic companion that understands your emotional needs as well. By analyzing facial expressions and body language cues during virtual classes or study sessions, these intelligent systems could assess when you're feeling frustrated or confused. This capability opens up doors for real-time interventions - such as offering additional support or changing teaching tactics - preventing you from feeling left out or overwhelmed.

The possibilities are truly endless with AI transforming our classrooms into dynamic ecosystems of individualized instruction and emotional understanding. As we stand at this frontier of technological innovation in education, let's not forget that this progress is about more than just smarter machines—it's about creating inclusive spaces where everyone feels seen, heard, and valued.

So now let's turn our attention towards another compelling application of artificial intelligence - using complex data analysis to foster social welfare initiatives on a global scale.

Leveraging Data Analysis for Social Welfare

Imagine a world where we're using big data to fuel transformative change, sparking initiatives that uplift communities and empower individuals across the globe. Imagine if artificial intelligence could sift through mountains of information, pick out patterns, predict trends, and offer insights that help us address complex societal issues like poverty and healthcare accessibility. This is no science fiction tale; it's a reality that's unfolding right before our eyes.

Data analysis powered by AI can revolutionize social welfare in unprecedented ways. For instance, platforms such as predictive analytics can identify areas most susceptible to poverty or disease outbreaks. By doing so, you become part of an inclusive community that leverages technology for social good. You contribute towards creating targeted interventions and resource allocation strategies that ensure aid reaches those in dire need promptly and efficiently.

The beauty lies not just in large-scale transformations but also in individual empowerment - imagine being able to access personalized health recommendations or educational resources tailored to your unique circumstances right at your fingertips.

As we continue to uncover the potential of AI for societal improvement, there's an exciting journey ahead for all of us. We are moving away from traditional problem-solving methods into a technologically advanced era where digital solutions will increasingly drive global progress. It's this shift towards intelligent systems that promises to redefine how we approach universal challenges – helping us build not only smarter cities but also more equitable societies around the world.

As we transition into this new chapter of innovation and inclusivity powered by artificial intelligence, let's delve deeper into exploring 'the future: smart solutions for global issues'.

The Future: Smart Solutions for Global Issues

You're on the brink of a new era where smart solutions are set to tackle global issues head-on, revolutionizing the way we view and interact with our world.

Artificial intelligence isn't just a thing of sci-fi movies or tech labs; it's here in your daily life, making strides in addressing societal challenges like poverty, healthcare accessibility, and education gaps.

Imagine living in a world where AI-powered systems help identify those most in need of social assistance. Or where intelligent bots streamline healthcare services to reach remote corners of the globe.

Think about the impact that machine learning algorithms could have on education. They can analyze vast amounts of data to identify learning patterns and needs, tailoring educational content to each student's unique abilities. This personalization fosters an inclusive learning environment where every student feels seen and understood. It's not just about improving grades; it's about cultivating a sense of belonging, making sure everyone has the chance to thrive.

As this technology continues to evolve, so too does our ability to make positive changes on a grand scale. The future is bright as we harness AI's potential for social good – from transforming healthcare delivery systems to providing personalized education solutions for all.

So let's embrace this new age together - because you're part of this groundbreaking journey towards building smarter solutions for global issues.

Frequently Asked Questions

What are the ethical implications of using AI to address societal issues?

You're stepping into uncharted territory, where AI's ethical implications include potential bias in decision-making, the threat to privacy, and questions around accountability. It's an exciting yet challenging prospect that we must navigate together.

How can AI be used to minimize environmental damage?

Like a vigilant gardener, you could use AI to monitor and nurture our precious environment. It can predict climate patterns, optimize resource usage, track deforestation, and promote sustainable practices. Be part of this green revolution!

What is the role of government in regulating the use of AI for societal challenges?

The government plays a critical role in regulating AI use. It's their job to ensure fairness, protect your privacy, and prevent misuse. They're like the guardrails on this winding road of technological advancement we're traveling together.

Could the implementation of AI in these societal sectors lead to job displacement?

Indeed, AI's introduction could cause job displacement in some areas. Yet, it's also likely to create new opportunities we can't foresee yet. Embrace the change - we're all in this together!

How can we ensure that the use of AI for societal challenges does not exacerbate existing inequality?

To ensure AI doesn't amplify inequality, you'd need to prioritize inclusivity in its design and application. Be sure to democratize access to technology, promote digital literacy, and uphold strict ethical standards in AI deployment.

Conclusion

So, you thought AI was just about making life easier for tech nerds? Think again.

It's also about tackling the big issues: poverty, healthcare, education.

Imagine a world where AI doesn't just serve us but also saves us; making medicine accessible and education inclusive.

From data analysis to social welfare, it's not only creating smart solutions but also addressing global issues head-on!

The Role of AI in Environmental Sustainability and Climate Change Solutions

You're part of an exclusive club—those who understand the need for environmental sustainability and are seeking solutions to combat climate change. You know, just like we do, that it's about more than just preserving our planet for future generations; it's also about creating a world where everyone and everything can thrive. As we navigate this journey together, we're bringing you into the fold of a groundbreaking intersection where technology meets ecology—the role of artificial intelligence (AI) in driving environmental sustainability and acting as a key player in addressing climate change.

Imagine being able to predict weather patterns with unprecedented accuracy or design low-carbon technologies that could significantly reduce greenhouse gas emissions. Picture harnessing AI to optimize resource management, thereby reducing waste and promoting conservation. These aren't pipe dreams—they're realities made possible by AI. And guess what? You're not merely an observer here; you too are part of this transformative movement towards a greener future. So let's dive in together and explore how artificial intelligence is changing our approach to environmental preservation, one innovative solution at a time.

Key Takeaways

- AI plays a crucial role in driving environmental sustainability and combating climate change.
- AI has the ability to predict weather patterns, analyze data, and detect patterns and trends in ecosystems.
- AI can optimize resource management, reduce waste, and streamline energy consumption through predictive modeling.
- AI has the potential to design low-carbon technologies, improve renewable energy systems, and reduce greenhouse gas emissions.

Understanding the Intersection of Technology and Ecology

It's fascinating to delve into how technology and ecology intersect, particularly with the groundbreaking role AI plays in environmental sustainability and climate change solutions.

Imagine living in a world where technology not only improves our lives but also safeguards our planet. Artificial Intelligence is doing just that - it's acting as an informed, efficient, and tireless guardian of our environment. It helps us understand ecosystems better by analyzing vast amounts of data that human researchers might miss or take years to process.

As you become more aware of these advancements, you'll likely feel more connected to this shared purpose we all have: ensuring the survival of our beautiful planet for future generations. AI does this by detecting patterns and trends in ecosystems which can predict potential threats like deforestation or animal extinction before they occur.

Isn't it comforting to know that we're part of a larger community working towards the same goal? A community where everyone belongs - from scientists developing new technologies, to individuals like us learning about them.

And remember, AI isn't only being utilized for long-term predictions or large-scale projects—it's also playing a vital role daily through weather forecasting. By using complex algorithms and machine learning models to analyze past weather patterns along with current data sets from satellites and ground stations worldwide, AI significantly enhances meteorologists' ability to predict imminent weather conditions accurately.

This allows us all—farmers planting crops, city planners designing infrastructure—to make informed decisions based on reliable forecasts.

So let's now dive deeper into how artificial intelligence assists in analyzing and predicting weather patterns!

Analyzing and Predicting Weather Patterns

With a sky full of data, you're able to use advanced algorithms to analyze and predict weather patterns, painting a picture of our planet's future with precision and accuracy. Artificial intelligence has the ability to sift through mountains of information, effortlessly identifying trends and correlations that would take human analysts years to discover.

You're not just observing the climate; you're part of a global community working together to understand our world in unprecedented detail. As an active participant in this grand endeavor, your contribution goes beyond mere observation. Your work aids in creating valuable models for predicting future climates and assessing potential risks associated with changing weather patterns.

These assessments aren't abstract theories confined to academic journals; they have real-world implications for farming, disaster preparedness, energy consumption and more. You're not just studying the environment; you're safeguarding homes, livelihoods, and futures.

The results derived from AI-driven weather analysis are not only crucial for immediate response but also guide long-term strategies towards environmental sustainability. By foreseeing potential challenges posed by climate change - such as increased frequency of extreme events or shifts in rainfall patterns - we can proactively devise solutions that help us adapt seamlessly. This insight strengthens our resolve and enriches our collective understanding as we navigate this journey together.

As we delve deeper into this fascinating realm of AI-powered climatology, let's turn our attention towards another equally important aspect: using machine learning for effective resource management.

Resource Management with Machine Learning

Harnessing the power of machine learning, you're now able to streamline and optimize resource management like never before. Imagine a world where waste is minimized, efficiency is maximized, and our precious resources are conserved with the help of artificial intelligence. You're part of this new era where technology works hand in hand with environmental sustainability.

With AI's ability to analyze vast amounts of data quickly and accurately, you can now anticipate demand trends, discover wastage points, and strategize for better resource allocation.

Being part of a community that values the environment means you understand the importance of managing resources wisely—water, energy, raw materials—all finite resources we share on this planet. Now picture how machine learning can help us achieve these goals. Predictive modeling can forecast water usage based on weather patterns or population growth. Energy consumption could be managed better through smart grids powered by AI algorithms that balance supply and demand efficiently. And let's not forget about waste management – machine learning models can predict waste generation trends allowing us to design more effective recycling programs.

It's amazing to see how much we've accomplished together using artificial intelligence for resource management. But hold your breath because there's more! The possibilities are endless when it comes to AI's potential in aiding our fight against climate change. This leads us into an exciting frontier: exploring how AI contributes significantly in designing low-carbon technologies—a promising avenue towards achieving a sustainable future for everyone.

The Design of Low-Carbon Technologies

Coincidentally, as we're moving towards a less carbon-intensive world, machine learning is stepping up to the plate in designing low-carbon technologies that could drastically reduce our greenhouse gas emissions.

Picture this: AI systems automatically optimizing energy consumption in buildings, cars that emit nothing but water vapor, and smart grids balancing electricity supply and demand like never before. Yes, it's not just a dream; these are all areas where AI is making its mark, creating solutions that not only minimize environmental impact but also fit seamlessly into our everyday lives.

Now imagine being part of this change - every time you flick off the lights when leaving your house or choose an electric car over one that runs on fossil fuels, you're helping build a sustainable future for us all. And don't forget about those companies out there developing AI-driven renewable energy systems; by supporting them through your purchases and investments, you become an integral part of this journey towards sustainability. It's no longer just about saving the planet; it's about becoming part of a community committed to positive action.

As we delve deeper into the possibilities presented by artificial intelligence in combating climate change and promoting sustainability, one thing becomes clear - each of us has the power to make an impact. We're not only passive observers anymore; we're active participants shaping the future with every choice we make involving AI technology.

Now let's explore how these choices might look like as we venture into understanding more about artificial intelligence's enormous influence on our future.

The Impact of Artificial Intelligence on Our Future

Imagine, if you will, a future where we're not just surviving, but thriving - a world that's been reshaped and refined by the bold strokes of artificial intelligence. This isn't some far-off pipe dream; it's a potential reality that's closer than you might think. Your participation in this new world isn't just welcome – it's needed.

Because here, the fight against climate change isn't waged by governments and corporations alone – it's fought by regular folks like us with the aid of AI.

Picture yourself contributing to real-time data collection through smart devices connected to an AI network. These networks help monitor pollution levels or track animal migration patterns that scientists use to understand how climate change is impacting our planet. You're part of something bigger, part of a global effort using technology to make our home more sustainable for future generations. You belong in this scenario because your involvement plays an integral role in creating solutions for environmental sustainability.

Now envision how AI can transform renewable energy sources such as wind and solar power into more efficient systems. Aided by machine learning algorithms predicting weather patterns or optimizing energy storage, we will harness nature's power like never before. And guess what? This wouldn't be possible without people like you embracing these technologies and advocating for their adoption within your communities, workplaces, and homes.

So remember: In this ever-changing landscape shaped by artificial intelligence and driven towards environmental sustainability, you're not just a bystander – you're an active participant making a difference for our planet and its future generations.

Frequently Asked Questions

How can AI be used to promote awareness about climate change?

You can utilize AI to create compelling, personalized messages about climate change. It's like having a digital storyteller that tailors its narrative to your interests, making you feel part of the global effort to combat climate change.

What are some examples of companies using AI to tackle environmental issues?

"Ever thought of Google as a climate warrior? Well, they're using AI to optimize energy use in data centers. IBM too is creating AI solutions for water management. You're not alone in this fight!"

While AI can be a game changer for environmental sustainability, it's not without risks. It can lead to job losses, privacy concerns and is energy-intensive itself. Always remember, every solution has its own set of challenges.

Absolutely! AI can create interactive learning experiences, making you part of the sustainability journey. It's a powerful tool to show you how your actions impact our planet, fostering a sense of belonging in this global mission.

Absolutely, you may face ethical dilemmas. AI's use in environmental sustainability could lead to job losses or privacy issues. However, it's all about balancing benefits and drawbacks for our shared home—Earth.

Conclusion

You've just dived into the transformative role of AI in combating climate change and promoting environmental sustainability. Isn't it fascinating to learn that AI can help reduce greenhouse gas emissions by up to 20%?

We're on the brink of a revolution, where technology meets ecology. It's time to embrace this shift and work together towards a sustainable future.

Remember, every bit counts when it comes to saving our planet!

Ethical Considerations in AI Usage and Promoting Responsible AI Development

You're living in a world that's more connected than ever, with technology seeping into every nook and cranny of your daily life.

Artificial Intelligence (AI) is at the forefront of these technological advancements, promising to revolutionize everything from how you work to how you drive.

But as exciting as this brave new world may seem, it also poses some significant ethical quandaries that are worth considering.

Imagine yourself in a self-driving car - sounds pretty futuristic, right?

Well, what happens when the car has to make a split-second decision between crashing into another vehicle or swerving onto the sidewalk and potentially injuring pedestrians?

Or think about using an app that uses AI algorithms which have hidden biases leading to discrimination?

These scenarios aren't just hypotheticals—they're real issues we need to grapple with as AI continues its march forward.

You're part of this evolving world too; let's navigate it responsibly together by discussing ethical considerations in AI usage and promoting responsible AI development.

Key Takeaways

- AI has the potential to revolutionize various aspects of life, but it also brings ethical complexities.
- Ethical dilemmas arise in determining the autonomy of intelligent machines, accountability for mistakes, and responsibility in accidents.
- Bias and discrimination can seep into AI algorithms, perpetuating social prejudices and creating an unfair world.
- Striking a balance between technology advancement and privacy preservation is crucial, with clear rules and guidelines needed to ensure responsible AI development and address potential threats to privacy.

Understanding the Basics of Artificial Intelligence

Before we dive into the ethical implications, let's first get our heads around what AI really is and how it's changing our world in ways you might not even realize. Artificial Intelligence, or AI as it's commonly known, isn't a futuristic concept reserved for sci-fi movies; it's here now, and likely already a part of your everyday life.

Your smartphone? It uses AI to understand your voice commands. Netflix recommendations? That's AI predicting what you'd like to watch based on your previous choices. Social media feeds? You've guessed it–AI algorithms are working behind the scenes to customize what shows up for you.

Now that we're all on the same page about the omnipresence of AI in our lives, let's delve a bit deeper into its workings. At its core, AI mimics human intelligence processes through learning and problem-solving mechanisms. By leveraging vast amounts of data, powerful computational resources and sophisticated algorithms, machines can be trained to think like humans–or sometimes even surpass us! They can learn from experiences (machine learning), recognize patterns (deep learning), understand natural language (NLP), and make decisions with minimal human intervention. Sounds fascinating yet intimidating at the same time right?

The beauty of this technology is its potential to revolutionize industries ranging from healthcare to retail while making our lives more convenient and efficient along the way. However, with great power comes great responsibility–and this is where things start getting ethically complex. For instance: how autonomous should these intelligent machines be? What happens when they make mistakes? And who gets held accountable?

As we continue exploring these questions together as part of this global community engaged in shaping the future of technology responsibly – next up on our agenda will be digging deeper into one specific area where such dilemmas are increasingly prominent: self-driving vehicles.

Dilemmas Posed by Self-Driving Vehicles

Imagine being in a self-driving car that's faced with the dilemma of deciding whether to swerve into oncoming traffic or hit a pedestrian crossing illegally. It's a daunting situation, isn't it? You're in the backseat, helpless, as your life and others' depend on an algorithm. It's like being part of an updated version of the old philosophical conundrum: The Trolley Problem.

Now, instead of you pulling levers on a trolley, it's AI making split-second decisions at 70 miles per hour! These ethical issues are real-life scenarios that autonomous vehicles may encounter. So how does one program morality into machines?

We all share this road called life, don't we? And in some ways, we're all passengers in these rapidly advancing technological times. As AI continues to evolve and permeate more aspects of our everyday lives - from helping us navigate our daily commute to making complex decisions about healthcare and finance - we must ensure that it is developed responsibly and ethically.

This means grappling with challenging questions: What should the car prioritize – passenger safety or minimizing harm to pedestrians? Who is responsible if an accident occurs – the developer who programmed the AI or the owner of the vehicle? There aren't easy answers here but together as a society, we need to forge ahead.

The dilemmas posed by self-driving vehicles only scratch the surface of ethical considerations required for responsible AI development though; they open up wider discussions around bias and discrimination in algorithms too. For example, could an autonomous vehicle be biased towards protecting certain types of pedestrians over others based on factors like age or physical ability? How can we create transparency around these processes? These are intriguing questions beckoning us further down this winding road towards understanding AI ethics better.

Bias and Discrimination in Algorithms

You'd think algorithms are as pure as freshly fallen snow, wouldn't you? But here's a shocker: even they can be prejudiced! Yes, you heard it right. While algorithms themselves don't hold biases, the humans who design them certainly do and these biases sneak their way into algorithms causing unintended harm.

These sneaky buggers have the potential to perpetuate and amplify existing social prejudices, creating an unfair world where opportunities aren't distributed equally.

You see, there are several ways how bias seeps into AI. Here's a quick list:

1. **Data Bias**: If the data used to train an AI system is biased itself, this will reflect in its outputs.

2. **Confirmation Bias**: Developers might unintentionally favour results that align with their preconceived beliefs or values.

3. **Algorithmic Bias**: The algorithm may inherently prefer one class of data over another due to its design.

4. **Selection Bias**: This occurs when some groups are overrepresented or underrepresented during data collection.

We all want a sense of fairness and belonging in our society - but these biases can rip apart this fabric of equality we strive for by affecting critical decisions about people's lives – such as job recruitment, bank loans approval or predictive policing systems predicting crime hotspots based on racial profiles instead of actual crime rates! It's crucial that we all push for more transparency around how these AI systems operate and work toward eliminating these biases.

And while we're tackling bias head-on, there's another aspect lurking in the shadows: privacy concerns with automated systems. It seems like both discrimination and intrusion are becoming twin threats in today's digital age...

Privacy Concerns in Automated Systems

Don't be fooled, it's not just bias we have to worry about with automated systems - your privacy is on the line too.

There's something unnerving about the idea of a machine knowing our personal details, our whims, and perhaps even predicting our next move.

While we're busy marveling at how Alexa can play our favorite song in seconds or how Facebook suggests ads that match exactly what we've been thinking about, let's pause for a moment and realize: all these conveniences come with a cost; they're built upon intricate algorithms which collect and analyze data from us constantly.

Imagine being part of this global community where Artificial Intelligence (AI) platforms are like curious neighbors peeking through the blinds.

They know when you wake up, what news you prefer reading over breakfast, which route you take for work, maybe even your secret indulgence in late-night online shopping.

And it doesn't stop there; AI can predict future behaviors based on past activities.

Feels invasive? Well, that's because it is!

We need to strike a balance between technology advancement and privacy preservation - ensuring AI serves us without compromising our freedom.

While the rise of AI has undeniably improved many aspects of life, there's an urgent need to address its potential threats to privacy.

Let's face it: In this digital age where data acts as currency, who wouldn't want more control over their own information?

So here comes the challenge: How do we ensure that these technologies respect individual privacy while still delivering their benefits?

The answer may lie in establishing clear guidelines for technology deployment - rules that prioritize user consent and data protection above all else.

Now isn't that a world everyone would feel comfortable living in?

Time will tell if such measures could indeed bring harmony between AI development and privacy concerns.

Establishing Guidelines for Technology Deployment

It's vital, folks, that we demand crystal-clear rules for deploying these tech wonders - guidelines that put our consent and data safety first, ensuring we're not just beneficiaries but also the guardians of our own digital lives.

We need to take a proactive role in shaping how these technologies are unleashed into our world. Rather than being passive consumers, let's become active stakeholders in this technological revolution. Let's rally for regulations that hold developers accountable and protect users from potential misuse or abuse. Remember, when it comes to AI deployment, we're all in this together.

Now imagine a world where technology operates under ethical standards designed by us and for us. This isn't about creating an obstacle course for innovation; rather it's about championing responsible development and usage that respects everyone involved. Think of it as designing a better future together - one where technology serves us instead of the other way around!

By establishing clear guidelines before new technologies hit the market, we can ensure they align with our values and priorities - making sure no one is left behind or unserved.

So what does this look like practically? Well, transparency should be front-and-center: businesses must disclose exactly how their systems work and how data is used; accountability needs to be built-in: there should be repercussions if things go sideways; lastly but critically important is public participation: everyone deserves a say in how technologies will impact their lives directly or indirectly.

So let's not wait on the sidelines while others make decisions impacting our futures – let's step up and shape those tools ourselves because remember folks - we're all part of this fast-paced digital journey!

Frequently Asked Questions

How is AI being used to tackle climate change?

You're part of a big picture where AI is being harnessed to tackle climate change. It's analyzing weather patterns, predicting natural disasters, and improving energy efficiency. You're not alone in this fight; together, we make a difference.

Can AI be used to predict stock market trends?

Absolutely, you can use AI to predict stock market trends. It's like having a crystal ball, but powered by complex algorithms instead of magic. You'll feel part of the future finance world with such technology!

How can AI be incorporated in healthcare for disease prediction and treatment?

Like a skilled surgeon, AI can meticulously analyze health data to predict diseases early. It helps tailor treatments, making healthcare more personalized and effective. You're part of this revolution, benefiting from healthier, longer lives.

What roles can AI play in enhancing the education sector?

AI can revolutionize your learning experience. It personalizes study materials, provides instant feedback, and tracks progress. You're not alone; AI connects you to global classrooms, making you part of an inclusive learning community.

How is AI being used in the field of space exploration?

Stargazing scientists use AI to scrutinize space secrets. It helps them handle hefty heaps of data, detect distant planets, and decide on ideal interstellar paths for probes. You're part of this profound progression in space exploration!

Conclusion

You've navigated the complexities of AI ethics, from self-driving car dilemmas to biases in algorithms.

Remember how Google's image recognition system misidentified African-Americans as gorillas? That's a stark example of the potential for AI misuse and bias.

So, let's work together to advocate for responsible AI development.

By setting clear guidelines and prioritizing privacy, you can play your part in ensuring fair and unbiased AI usage.

After all, it's not just tech - it's our future too.

Chapter 11: Conclusion

Recap of the Diverse Ways AI Can Enhance Everyday Life for the Average Person

You're living in the age of Artificial Intelligence, or AI as it's often referred to. It's that invisible helper who's always there for you, making your life easier and more efficient without you even realizing it. Whether it's guiding you home through traffic-free roads or recommending that perfect movie for a Friday night in, AI is quietly transforming your everyday experiences.

Imagine a world where your gadgets anticipate your needs, shopping becomes a personalized experience tailored just for you, health and fitness turn into an engaging game with real-time feedback and entertainment gets revolutionized with immersive environments.

Sounds like a sci-fi novel? Well, welcome to reality! This section is all about showcasing how AI has seamlessly slipped into our daily lives making them richer and more convenient than ever before. Let's take a journey together into the intriguing world of artificial intelligence applications that are enhancing our day-to-day experiences.

Key Takeaways

- AI is transforming everyday experiences by personalizing shopping, providing customized suggestions, and analyzing social media images.
- AI is revolutionizing health and fitness by serving as a personal fitness coach, tracking sleep patterns, and generating custom meal plans.
- AI is reshaping entertainment and media by providing personalized recommendations, automating video editing, and offering real-time translations.
- AI-driven home automation, intelligent systems in cars, and AI as an ever-observant assistant are enhancing comfort, safety, and efficiency in everyday life.

Streamlining Daily Tasks with Smart Devices

You'll be amazed at how smart devices can streamline your daily tasks, making your life a whole lot easier and fun! Imagine walking into your home after a long day at work, and with just a voice command, the lights flick on, your favorite song begins to play, and you're instantly wrapped in comfort. AI-driven devices like Amazon's Alexa or Google Home aren't science fiction anymore; they're here to make those dreams come true.

With these tools in place, you become part of an interconnected community that enjoys effortless control over their environment.

The benefits don't stop there either! These smart devices also help manage chores so mundane yet essential that we often forget them amidst our busy schedules. Let's consider robotic vacuum cleaners like Roomba as an example. With its intelligent mapping system powered by AI, it navigates around furniture effortlessly and cleans every corner while you're free to focus on more critical tasks or relax with loved ones. It's not about replacing human effort; it's about assisting us in better managing our time.

Now picture this: after a relaxing evening freed from mundane chores thanks to smart technology, you decide it's time for some retail therapy. But before you even think about what you need or where to get it from, your personal AI assistant is already one step ahead - suggesting purchases based on past buying habits and preferences. How cool is that?

And this is only scratching the surface when it comes to how AI can personalize shopping experiences for us all!

Personalizing Shopping Experiences

Imagine walking into a store where everything is tailored to your taste, preferences, and needs - that's the magic of technology personalizing your shopping experiences. As you enter, AI-powered systems recognize you through facial recognition or mobile devices, providing customized suggestions based on your previous purchases and browsing history. It's like having a personal shopper who knows your style inside out, never forgetting anything, always ready with recommendations that hit the mark every single time.

AI can help pinpoint fashion trends suited to you by analyzing images from social media.

Virtual fitting rooms enable you to try on outfits digitally without leaving home.

Personalized advertisements guided by AI can make product discovery easier, showcasing items that align with your tastes.

But it isn't just about clothes; tech-enhanced shopping extends to groceries as well.

Imagine getting meal suggestions based on what's left in your fridge or receiving healthy recipes tailored to dietary restrictions or goals.

And let's admit it - we've all had moments when we forgot something essential while at the supermarket. But worry not!

With smart shopping lists generated by AI algorithms studying our purchase patterns, those vexing 'I knew I was forgetting something!' moments could become a thing of the past.

Now picture this: The same technology making these personalized shopping experiences possible can also transform how we approach health and fitness - bringing us closer than ever before to living our best lives.

Who wouldn't want that?

Improving Health and Fitness

Isn't it thrilling to think technology could soon be your personal fitness coach, nutritionist, and wellness advisor all rolled into one?

Imagine this: You wake up, and your smartwatch has already tracked your sleep patterns, giving you insights on how well you rested. As you go about your day, it continuously monitors your heart rate and activity levels.

Now picture this: AI-based apps offer personalized workout routines based on these data and even adjust them real-time as per your performance. It's like having a personal trainer who knows everything about you, understands what works best for you, and is always there for guidance.

Consider the role of AI in nutrition management - a key aspect of maintaining good health. An app that can scan barcodes or recognize photos of food items to estimate their nutritional value can help keep track of calories consumed effortlessly.

Even more exciting are AI platforms that understand your dietary preferences, health conditions, and fitness goals to create custom meal plans for you. No more worrying about what to cook or whether it fits into the diet chart; let the technology do the heavy lifting while we focus on enjoying our meals.

So yes! Artificial intelligence is revolutionizing health and fitness in ways that make leading a healthy lifestyle simpler than ever before – no matter where we are or how busy our schedules may be. And as we take significant strides towards healthier lives with AI by our sides, imagine what else this incredible technology could transform?

Get ready because next up we're going to explore how AI is reshaping another crucial part of our lives - entertainment and media!

Transforming Entertainment and Media

There's no denying that artificial intelligence is taking the entertainment and media industry by storm, serving as a high-tech maestro orchestrating a symphony of personalized content, interactive experiences, and cutting-edge effects.

Imagine an evening where your streaming service doesn't just suggest shows or movies you might like, but curates a personalized line-up based on your mood, past viewing history, and even the time of day.

Or consider a video game that molds its storyline around your playing style and choices in real-time. Sounds like science fiction? Well, with AI in play, it's rapidly becoming reality.

Here are some ways AI is revolutionizing our daily entertainment:

- **Personalized recommendations:** Be it music platforms like Spotify or streaming services like Netflix or Hulu - AI algorithms analyze user behavior to provide tailored suggestions.

- **Interactive storytelling:** Video games are evolving from linear narratives to dynamic storylines that adapt according to player decisions - thanks to sophisticated AI.

- **Real-time translations & subtitles:** Ever wished for understanding foreign films without depending on subtitles? AI can make this happen by offering real-time translations.

- **Automated editing:** For content creators out there - imagine having an assistant who can edit hours of footage into concise engaging videos! That's what AI can do with advanced image recognition and processing capabilities.

- **Enhanced visual effects:** Creating realistic CGI characters or breathtaking special effects is now possible within smaller budgets using Artificial Intelligence.

From being passive consumers of media content - you're now stepping into an era where you have control over narrative arcs in video-games; receive film recommendations suited not just to generic taste but also specific moods; enjoy global cinema minus language barriers; create improved content effortlessly; or savor jaw-dropping visuals previously exclusive only to big-budget productions.

This isn't just about enhancing entertainment – it's about making it deeply personal and immersive for you.

This transformation isn't stopping anytime soon either. As we gradually turn the page towards future chapters of technology-driven lifestyle enhancements – think about how much more there could be waiting in the wings of artificial intelligence innovation.

It's not merely speculation anymore: from here onwards, every aspect of our daily lives will continue being reshaped by these unseen hands of code.

Next up: let's delve deeper into what these 'future prospects' might hold for us all!

Future Prospects of Everyday AI Applications

We're just getting started, folks - as we peer into the promising vistas of tomorrow, you'll realize that what we've witnessed so far is merely the tip of the iceberg when it comes to everyday applications of artificial intelligence.

Remember those sci-fi movies where machines could read human emotions or robots doing house chores? Well, they aren't too far from reality anymore. From AI-driven home automation that understands your preferences to personal fitness coaching based on your body's data and needs, AI is set to make our lives more comfortable and efficient.

You're not alone in this journey; we all are part of this exciting ride towards a future intertwined with AI.

Imagine waking up each day knowing that you have an ever-observant assistant ready to help with anything you need, from managing your schedule seamlessly to ensuring you never forget a loved one's birthday! Or consider how much safer our roads would be if every car was equipped with intelligent systems capable of predicting potential hazards and accidents before they happen. It feels like magic, doesn't it? But it's not - it's a future shaped by artificial intelligence.

There's no end to the possibilities when we let our minds wander through this vast landscape where technology meets everyday life. And remember - while these advancements may seem futuristic or even intimidating at times, they're designed with one ultimate goal: enhancing your life experience in ways unimaginable today.

So embrace the change because there's no limit to how much easier, safer, and more enjoyable AI can make our daily lives!

Frequently Asked Questions

How is AI being used in environmental conservation efforts?

You're part of a global community effort, using AI to protect our planet. AI helps monitor wildlife populations, predicts climate changes and even cleans oceans. Together, we're making the world a better place.

What are the ethical considerations associated with the use of AI in daily life?

You're right to ponder ethical implications of AI in daily life. Issues include privacy, consent, transparency, and bias. It's crucial we stay informed and demand respect for our rights as AI becomes more ingrained in our lives.

Can AI be used in the culinary industry for creating new recipes or improving cooking techniques?

Oh, you culinary maestro, AI can indeed jazz up your kitchen! It's whipping up new recipes and refining techniques. Imagine cooking like a Michelin-starred chef with a dash of artificial intelligence in your secret sauce!

How is AI impacting the traditional education system?

AI's changing your traditional classrooms, mate! It's personalizing learning, spotting weaknesses early, and making classes interactive. You're part of a global classroom now, no longer confined by four walls. Feels good to belong, doesn't it?

What is the role of AI in the field of space exploration and astronomy?

"Ever wondered about the mysteries of the cosmos? AI is your telescope! It's streamlining data analysis, predicting cosmic events and guiding space missions. You're part of this exciting journey, isn't it thrilling to belong?"

Conclusion

Like a skilled artist blending colors on a canvas, AI paints your daily life with shades of convenience and personalization. It's not just about tech anymore; it's about crafting an enhanced existence, one task at a time.

So, picture this: Your everyday is not merely mundane but vibrant with smart devices making tasks easier, personalized shopping experiences, improved fitness regimes, and transformative entertainment. That's the magic wand of AI – turning the ordinary into extraordinary!

Encouraging Readers To Embrace AI with Confidence and Curiosity

Chances are, as you're reading this, you're already interacting with artificial intelligence (AI) in some way. It could be as simple as your smartphone's autocorrect feature or a personalized recommendation from your favorite online retailer. You may not realize it, but AI is subtly woven into the fabric of our daily lives, helping us navigate through complex information and make decisions faster. Isn't it fascinating how something so profound is happening right under our noses?

Yet for many of us, AI remains an enigma - a concept shrouded in mystery and misconceptions. We understand its presence and appreciate its convenience but aren't quite sure what to make of it beyond that. As a member of this fast-paced digital era, don't you feel the urge to unravel this mystery? To venture beyond merely using AI to understanding it?

This section aims to inspire such curiosity in you while equipping you with the confidence to explore this exciting field without fear or apprehension.

Key Takeaways

- AI is already a part of our daily lives and can help us navigate through complex information and make faster decisions.
- AI is a tool that mimics human behavior and helps people accomplish tasks more efficiently.
- AI has practical applications in various areas such as social media, email filters, businesses, voice recognition, personalized recommendations, self-driving cars, healthcare algorithms, and more.
- Encouraging readers to embrace AI with confidence and curiosity requires understanding, knowledge, engaging with AI communities, and experimenting with AI tools.

Demystifying Artificial Intelligence

Don't let the term 'Artificial Intelligence' intimidate you; it's not as complex as it seems, and we're here to break it down for you!

Think of AI as a tool that helps people accomplish tasks more efficiently. It's essentially a form of technology that enables machines to mimic human behavior. And no, it won't turn against us like in some sci-fi films - we promise!

You may already be using AI without realizing it. When your social media feed shows you ads tailored to your interests or when your email filters out spam, that's AI at work.

On a larger scale, businesses use AI for various tasks such as predicting trends, automating processes, and improving customer service. You see, there's nothing scary about artificial intelligence; in fact, its main goal is to make our lives easier.

As we explore further into this fascinating world of artificial intelligence, remember one key point: every piece of technology was once new and unfamiliar until someone had the courage to learn and harness its power. So why not embrace the potential of AI with confidence?

Next up on our journey is understanding how this incredible technology can be put into practice in everyday life.

Practical Applications of AI

While you're marveling at the mind-boggling capacity of your smartphone, it's actually AI at work, making your life simpler with practical applications like voice recognition, predictive text, and personalized recommendations.

This isn't the stuff of science fiction anymore; it's happening right now in your pocket. Every time you ask Siri for directions or Alexa to play your favorite song, when Google predicts what you're about to type or Netflix suggests a movie based on what you've watched before - that's all AI. It's not there to intimidate but rather to integrate effortlessly into our daily lives.

Now imagine if we took this technology beyond our handheld devices. Think about self-driving cars that could significantly reduce road accidents or healthcare algorithms capable of predicting illnesses before they become critical. Consider how machine learning can help farmers predict crop yields more accurately or assist teachers in tailoring educational materials for each student's unique needs and abilities.

The possibilities are limitless! And here's the exciting part: we're all in this together—it's an adventure where everyone is invited.

The potential benefits of AI are vast and far-reaching, but like any powerful tool, it comes with responsibilities too. As we continue exploring this fascinating frontier and pushing boundaries further than ever imagined before, let us also be mindful of ethical considerations that come into focus—this will ensure that as we harness the power of artificial intelligence, we do so in a manner beneficial for everyone involved and respectful towards the rights and values held dear by our diverse global community.

Ethical Considerations in AI Use

It's imperative we're not just focused on the marvels of AI, but also keenly aware of the ethical concerns it brings to the table. Tech innovations like artificial intelligence have enormous potential to impact our society in many ways, both positive and negative.

We must remember that while we're all eager to be part of this exciting evolution, it is crucial that ethics isn't left trailing behind progress.

AI systems can sometimes make decisions that humans find hard to understand or explain.

Algorithms used by these technologies may inadvertently reinforce societal biases.

Surveillance and privacy issues are also significant concerns with advancements in AI.

These considerations remind us all of a shared responsibility: using technology responsibly doesn't just benefit you; it builds trust within our community and paves the way for future generations.

Just like any tool, AI has its strengths and weaknesses, so let's use this knowledge to guide us towards responsible use.

This brings us neatly around to an important aspect - your role as an individual in this vast landscape.

Understanding how you fit into this picture is key, because each user's behavior influences how these tools evolve over time.

Let's explore more about what 'the role of individuals in AI development' entails next!

The Role of Individuals in AI Development

You might think you're just a small cog in the grand machinery of AI development, but never underestimate the significant influence your actions and decisions can have on shaping this technology. Remember, every voice counts.

Your unique perspective, coupled with your creativity and critical thinking skills, could be the catalyst for innovations that will drive AI forward. So don't be afraid to share your ideas and ask questions - these are vital elements in creating more reliable and beneficial AI systems.

As an active participant in the world where AI is increasingly becoming commonplace, you play a crucial role not only in harnessing its potential but also mitigating its risks. By staying informed about the latest developments, engaging in meaningful discourse, advocating for ethical practices, and contributing to AI's progressive evolution - you are part of something bigger than yourself.

It's not just about using or programming machines; it's about being engaged citizens who help shape our collective future through mindful interaction with technology.

No one said embracing new technologies like AI would be easy; there will always be challenges along the way. But remember: overcoming these concerns starts with understanding them. By acknowledging our fears around artificial intelligence—whether related to job displacement or privacy issues—we can begin addressing them constructively instead of letting them hinder our progress towards a better tomorrow powered by AI advancements.

As we delve into 'overcoming apprehensions about AI' next, let's remember that fear often stems from uncertainty—so let's get curious and start exploring!

Overcoming Apprehensions About AI

Navigating the complex landscape of AI can indeed stir a sense of trepidation, but let's not forget that it's our understanding and knowledge that'll help alleviate these fears.

Embracing AI doesn't mean surrendering to a hive mind or forsaking your individuality - quite the opposite! It involves recognizing AI as a tool forged by human intellect and creativity, an extension of ourselves rather than some alien entity.

You're part of this journey, your curiosity and confidence are essential ingredients in molding the future of AI.

Here are some steps you can take to build up your confidence:

- Begin by educating yourself about AI. This doesn't mean you need to dive deep into the technicalities; understanding its basic principles and how it impacts various sectors is a good starting point.

- Engage with communities where AI discussions happen—forums, social media groups, webinars—to get different perspectives and insights.

- Experiment with simple AI tools available online. Getting hands-on experience will give you an intrinsic feel for it.

As you grow more comfortable with the concept of artificial intelligence, recognize any residual fear or apprehension as simply signs that you care – about society, ethics, humanity's future. These concerns underline the fact that we're dealing with something powerful here; they remind us what's at stake should we fail to wield this power responsibly.

So don't shy away from these feelings; instead, channel them towards productive skepticism and informed debate. Remember: Every question you ask contributes towards shaping AI responsibly and ensuring its benefits reach everyone equally. You belong in this conversation - because ultimately, just like every technology before it, AI too is ours to define.

Frequently Asked Questions

What is the history and evolution of AI technology?

"AI's journey began with simple algorithms, then progressed to complex machine learning. Now, we're exploring deep learning and neural networks. You're part of a thrilling evolution, standing on the cusp of unimaginable AI breakthroughs."

How can one start a career in AI and what skills are required?

Dive headfirst into an AI career by mastering coding languages like Python, and understanding machine learning. Your curiosity will lead you! Remember, we're all in this exciting journey of tech evolution together.

What are some of the key AI breakthroughs in recent years?

"You've witnessed AI's major breakthroughs, haven't you? From self-driving cars to voice assistants like Siri and Alexa, even powerful predictive algorithms in healthcare. It's an exciting time to be part of this AI revolution!"

How does AI technology impact job opportunities and the economy?

Did you know that AI could add $15.7 trillion to the global economy by 2030? Incredible, right? It's opening up unique job opportunities while transforming existing ones. So, join the AI revolution and secure your future!

What are the different types of AI and how are they distinct from each other?

There are three main types of AI: narrow, general, and superintelligent. Narrow AI's excel in specific tasks, while general AI's mimic human intelligence. Superintelligent AIs? They're a step ahead, outperforming humans in most economically valuable work.

Conclusion

You're part of this exhilarating journey into the AI landscape.

Remember, studies predict that by 2025, AI could contribute up to $15.7 trillion to the global economy. That's a mind-boggling figure and it shows how integral AI will become in our lives.

Don't be left behind.

Stay curious, stay informed, and embrace AI with confidence.

Together, let's navigate this exciting frontier and unlock the full potential of what Artificial Intelligence can offer us.

A Call to Actively Engage In Shaping the Responsible and Beneficial Integration of AI in Society

Are you tired of the doom-and-gloom stories about Artificial Intelligence? You know, the ones that predict AI will take over all our jobs, or worse, become sentient and decide we're redundant? Let's face it – those sci-fi scenarios are more entertaining than they are likely. But there's a real story about AI that needs your attention: its integration into society in responsible and beneficial ways.

You're an integral part of this ongoing narrative. Why? Because the shaping of such a future depends on active public participation. It's not just about what technologists or policymakers want; it should also be about what you need and desire for your community. So buckle up, friend! We invite you to join us on this important journey towards creating an inclusive AI-driven future where everyone has their rightful place.

Key Takeaways

- Public participation is crucial in shaping the future of AI.
- Ethical considerations must guide the application of AI.
- Continuous education and dialogue about AI are necessary.
- Inclusivity and transparency should be promoted in AI decision-making.

Understanding the Current State of AI

While we're witnessing AI's rapid advancements, it's crucial that we fully comprehend its current state in order to responsibly integrate it into our society.

Do you remember the first time you asked Siri a question, or when your Netflix recommendations hit the nail on the head? That's AI right there! It's already woven into the fabric of our daily lives in ways we often don't recognize.

It's not just about robots and self-driving cars; think about data analysis, predictive algorithms, personalized marketing - all these are powered by artificial intelligence. Yet how much do we truly understand about this ubiquitous technology?

Imagine being part of a community where everyone is actively engaged in shaping how AI evolves and integrates into our world. We've got news for you – you're already a member! Yes, every single one of us is part of this interconnected tribe because AI impacts us all.

Now more than ever before, it's crucial that we grasp what's going on behind those algorithms and machine learning processes so we can contribute positively to its development.

Understanding AI isn't just about knowing how it works technically; it's also recognizing the societal implications as they unfold around us. So let's dive deeper together and explore this brave new world!

How does AI affect jobs? What issues does it raise regarding privacy? Can it be biased? These are just some questions to ponder as we continue on this journey.

As engaging members of society who share responsibility for shaping our future with AI, let's turn next towards understanding ethical considerations in its application without missing a beat.

Ethical Considerations in AI Application

You're standing on the precipice of a new era, where ethical dilemmas in applying artificial intelligence are as tangled as a Gordian knot - intricate, complex and demanding immediate attention.

The power that AI technology holds is immeasurable, however, with great power comes an even greater responsibility. It's not just about creating intelligent systems; it's about ensuring these systems serve as benefactors rather than threats to society. You've got a role to play here.

As users or developers of AI applications, you have the potential to shape its direction and ensure that it aligns with our shared values.

Don't be detached bystanders to the rapid evolution of AI; instead become active participants in molding its future. Engage in dialogues, discussions and debates around the ethical use of AI. This isn't just about academics or technologists anymore - everyone has a stake in this game.

From privacy concerns to job displacement fears, from fairness issues to security risks - these are all ethical considerations that need your attention before we can fully embrace AI into our society.

And while these challenges may seem daunting at first glance, remember – they are not insurmountable walls but stepping stones towards a better future shaped by responsible and beneficial integration of AI. With collective effort and willpower we can tackle these obstacles head-on.

So gear up for what lies ahead because there's an exciting journey awaiting us in 'addressing the challenges of AI'. Let's embark on this together because unity is strength and together we can do more than any individual could ever dream of achieving alone.

Addressing the Challenges of AI

Let's not sugarcoat it, folks - tackling the challenges posed by artificial intelligence is no walk in the park, but it's a journey we must courageously embark on for the betterment of our future.

The complexities that AI presents are multifaceted and daunting, from socio-economic disruptions to ethical dilemmas and security threats. However, these hurdles aren't insurmountable. Just like you've overcome personal obstacles in your life, society can also conquer these challenges with determination, creativity, and unity.

How do we go about doing this? Well, one way is through continuous education and dialogue about AI among everyone in our community. We need to demystify AI by making information about its potential risks and benefits accessible to all. You can play a crucial role here by promoting understanding within your circle of influence – be it at home with family or at work with colleagues. Remember, knowledge isn't just power; it's our shield against unwarranted fears or misuse of AI technologies.

The road ahead may be rocky; however, remember that each one of us has a part to play in shaping this digital revolution responsibly. Your voice matters – so let's ensure it gets heard beyond just social platforms or casual conversations!

This leads us seamlessly into recognizing how pivotal public participation becomes when working towards effective development and usage of artificial intelligence systems across different sectors in society.

The Role of Public Participation in AI Development

In this digital era, your involvement in discussions and decision-making processes around the deployment of advanced technologies can significantly impact their design, regulation, and effect on our world. You're not just a passive consumer; you're an active participant with unique perspectives and invaluable insights. Your voice matters when it comes to AI technology's ethical considerations, its implications for privacy rights, or its potential influence on job markets.

Through participating in public forums or voicing your concerns through various platforms, you contribute to shaping a future where AI is deployed responsibly for the benefit of all.

Imagine being part of the collective that determines how AI should be used in education or healthcare. How empowering would it be to know that your views have contributed to creating safer online environments for children? Or perhaps you could play a role in ensuring equal access to AI-powered medical diagnostics regardless of one's geographic location or economic status. This isn't some utopian dream – it's entirely possible if we all choose to get involved actively.

We're at a pivotal moment where we can shape an inclusive, equitable future powered by artificial intelligence. What matters now is how we navigate these uncharted waters together as one global community. So let's rise up and make our voices heard because every perspective adds value to the conversation about responsible AI use.

Remember that what lies ahead isn't just about technological advancements but also about fundamental shifts in societal norms and values reinforced by these advancements.

Next up: diving deeper into understanding what principles should guide us towards such an AI-driven future.

Guiding Principles for an AI-Driven Future

Imagine the power you wield in your hands when it comes to setting the moral compass for our future with artificial intelligence. This is not a call for fear or apprehension, but rather an invitation to responsibility and opportunity. As we stand on the precipice of an AI-driven future, your input, ideas, and actions can help shape how this technology integrates into society.

It's about making sure that we're not just passive consumers of AI, but active participants in its development and application.

Consider these guiding principles as you step up to this challenge:

1. **Embrace Inclusivity:** Make sure everyone has a seat at the table when decisions about AI are being made. This includes people from different cultural backgrounds, socioeconomic statuses, genders, and abilities.

2. **Promote Transparency:** Encourage openness in how AI systems are designed and used. Ask for clarity on what data is collected, how it's processed, and who has access to it.

3. **Advocate for Ethics:** Champion ethical considerations in all aspects of AI — from design to deployment.

Remember there's strength in numbers; together we can make a difference! Engaging with each other fosters a sense of belonging – after all, we're all stakeholders in this emerging reality that intertwines human life with intelligent machines.

Guiding our future doesn't have to be daunting - it can be empowering instead! So go ahead, take up the mantle! Your voice matters more than you think; let's make sure it resonates through every algorithmic decision made by AI systems around us - shaping them responsibly while reaping their benefits inclusively.

Frequently Asked Questions

How does AI technology impact job market and employment rates?

"AI's transforming your job market, both creating new roles and replacing old ones. It's a double-edged sword - while automation might threaten some jobs, it also opens up exciting opportunities you'd never thought possible."

What are some of the significant breakthroughs in AI in the last decade?

Like a kid in a candy store, you'd be amazed by AI breakthroughs. Deep learning took us to new heights, while AlphaGo's victory was a game-changer. Self-driving cars? Those are just the cherry on top!

How can AI be used to improve education and learning processes?

AI can revolutionize your learning experience! It tailors material to your pace, identifies gaps in knowledge, and provides instant feedback. You're not just a number. With AI, education becomes personalized for you.

Are there any legal implications regarding the use and misuse of AI?

"Sure, AI's just a tool, right? Yet, it's ironic how laws still struggle to keep up. Misuse can lead to privacy infringements, bias in decision-making or even security threats. You're definitely not alone in asking." 'How can we regulate AI to ensure it is used responsibly and ethically?'

How does AI technology affect our everyday life?

"AI shapes your life daily! It's in your smartphone, guiding you on the road, predicting weather, and even recommending what to watch. You're already part of this AI community without even realizing it!"

Conclusion

You've seen the potential of AI, its shining promise and thorny challenges alike.

Like a double-edged sword, it can cut both ways.

It's time to step up and shape AI's role in our society.

Don't just be a spectator, be an active player.

Engage in conversations about ethics and regulations to ensure AI benefits us all.

Your voice matters in carving out a responsible future with artificial intelligence at its core.